SWIFT'S POLITE CONVERSATION

Swift's
Polite Conversation

with Introduction,
Notes and Extensive Commentary by

ERIC PARTRIDGE

ANDRE DEUTSCH

FIRST PUBLISHED 1963 BY
ANDRE DEUTSCH LIMITED
105 GREAT RUSSELL STREET
LONDON W C I
COPYRIGHT © 1963 BY ERIC PARTRIDGE
ALL RIGHTS RESERVED
PRINTED IN GREAT BRITAIN BY
TONBRIDGE PRINTERS LTD
TONBRIDGE KENT

827

For my friends at the University of Minnesota:

John W. Clark
Samuel H. Monk
Franz Montgomery
Robert E. Moore
Robert Stange

good scholars and good fellows:
gratefully from the editor
who, cheerfully and indeed unavoidably,
remains in their debt

CONTENTS

	page
Preface	9
The Editor's General Introduction	11
Swift's Introduction to *Polite Conversation*	21
Notes on Swift's Introduction	43
Swift's *Polite Conversation* In Three Dialogues *with the Editor's Commentary on the Dialogues*	49
Index of Subjects including Persons and Book-Titles	179

PREFACE

It has often been pointed out that historians and students of English owe much to Swift for his shrewd remarks and observations, made on several occasions, upon the language; and writers treating of English style have, almost *ad nauseam,* told us of the numerous excellences displayed in his prose works. I hardly care to labour the obvious.

I merely intend to show, not by theory but by practice, how alert the master is – how quick and sensitive his ear – how retentive his memory – how exact his transcripts – in the three dialogues that go to form his running commentary on the polite conversation of the early eighteenth century : and I do this by means of a running commentary.

To do it at all, it was necessary to use the best text; in short, that prepared by Professor Herbert Davis for the Blackwell edition of Swift's prose works. To Sir Basil Blackwell and Professor Davis I am most grateful for their prompt and generous permission.

In the comments upon proverbs and proverbial phrases, I have – like everyone else – had to lean heavily upon G. L. Apperson's *English Proverbs and Proverbial Phrases,* 1929, and *The Oxford Dictionary of English Proverbs,* second edition, revised by Sir Paul Harvey, 1948 : my references are to 'Apperson' and 'ODEP'. In catch-phrases, although a few are recorded in those two authorities, I have often been obliged to resort to *A Dictionary of Slang and Unconventional English,* fifth edition, 1961 (DSUE). 'OED' is – of course – *The Oxford English Dictionary.*

ERIC PARTRIDGE

THE EDITOR'S GENERAL INTRODUCTION

Jonathan Swift (1667–1745) deserves from all historians, students and lovers of English a gratitude much deeper, a praise much higher, than he has ever received – except perhaps from the genial and erudite George Saintsbury, who, despite an apparent quirkiness, possessed a remarkably sound judgement and who, surrounded by an infinity of trees, could always measure and appreciate and display the forest.

Swift, whose own prose style was, at its best, lucid, direct, immensely effective, retained throughout his adult years a passion for the purity and simplicity of English style and for the purity and value of the English language. I have more than once seen it stated and heard it said that, in his essays and papers on English vocabulary and syntax and style, whether written or spoken, he was never profound : but in which of the half-dozen or so essays and papers dealing with English would profundity have been necessary or even suitable? The *Discourse* is a savagely ironic and often burlesque attack on the pedants; the *Proposal* was addressed to a busy politician and preoccupied statesman; the remaining pieces were intentionally light in both matter and manner.

Rather than adversely criticize Swift for what he did not even attempt, let us generously acclaim him for what he did, and fully intended to, achieve. Into the stuffy atmosphere that, with one exception, had pervaded the attitude towards, hence the treatment of, English and was, with very few exceptions, to pervade it for many years to come, Swift brought a breath of cool, fresh air, a shrewd appreciation of the facts as opposed to the theory of the spoken and written language, and a judgement at once conservative and forward-looking. Dryden might conceivably have done this, but he too soon became a pontiff, something Swift was fundamentally too modest to become.

If we take the relevant essays and other works mainly in the order of their publication, we have first to consider the essay in *The Tatler* (No. 230) of 28 September 1710, despite the fact that *Polite Conversation* was at least begun some six years earlier. In the *Tatler* essay, Swift wittily attacks certain 'false refinements', especially such truncations as *mob, phiz, pozz, rep,* and such slang as *banter* and *bamboozle,* and then pleads for the introduction, into our style, of 'that simplicity which is the best and truest ornament of most things in human life'; by simplicity he intended his readers to understand neither baldness nor flatness nor a pedestrian monotony. In *A History of Criticism* (1900-1904), George Saintsbury has truly said that 'the famous *Tatler* . . ., on the conceptions of English style and writing, ought to hold place in every history and course of lectures on the subject, next to Sprat's passage in the *History of the Royal Society* forty years before, as the manifesto of a fresh stage in English style-criticism; and it practically precedes everything that Addison, Steele, and Pope published on, or in connecton with, the subject'.

A Proposal for Correcting, Improving and Ascertaining the English Tongue appeared two years later. Although its author disclaimed any political intention, he associated himself closely with the Tory party and went rather out of his way to eulogize Harley, 'Lord High Treasurer of Great Britain'. Nevertheless, he did genuinely advocate the formation of an academy, corresponding to the Académie Française and designed especially to correct and settle the language, 'that we may not perpetually be changing as we do'; he was, of course, far from being the first Briton to propose such an academy. By settling the language, he did not, however, mean that, after being corrected, it should undergo no changes at all. Indeed, he clearly says : 'I do not mean that it should never be enlarged : Provided, that no Word, which a Society' – the proposed academy – 'shall give a Sanction to, be afterwards antiquated and exploded, they may have Liberty to receive whatever new ones they shall find Occasion for : Because then the old Books will yet be always valuable according to their intrinsick Worth, and not thrown aside on Account of unintelligible Words and Phrases, which appear harsh and uncouth, only because they are out of Fashion'. He was, in short, pleading for the establishment of a Standard, not a fossilized, English.

Letter to a Young Gentleman, Lately entered into Holy Orders – usually known as *Letter to a Young Clergyman* – was published in 1720. It is Swift's 'most important pronouncement on style', as Professor Bonamy Dobrée has remarked in his valuable *English Literature in the Early Eighteenth Century*. 'But,' he adds, 'it is sometimes forgotten that Swift was suggesting rules for a spoken composition . . . He is not pretending to cover style as a whole.' The 'spoken composition' Swift had in mind is the sermon : for which, he says, 'Proper words in proper Places, makes the true Definition of a Stile'. This *Letter* is notable for its abundant good sense.

Written some time after 1727, but unpublished until 1765, was *A Discourse to Prove the Antiquity of the English Tongue,* 'a sort of learned joke, a parody of philological scholarship', as Professor Herbert Davis has called it. True; and much of it consists of nothing more dignified than 'a game of playing with Greek and Latin names'. It does, however, contain a salutary condemnation of 'those scholars who claim approbation for the long years of labour which they have undertaken for the benefit of mankind and for the honour of their own dear country' – to adopt Professor Davis's Swiftian summary. Saintsbury has summarized the *Discourse* rather differently; yet, in the main, similarly: 'Though all persons with a true English appreciation of shameless puns and utter nonsense must delight in *The Antiquity of the English Tongue,* it cannot be called serious criticism'.

Not long before his fierce spirit and noble mind became distorted and darkened, Swift at last in 1738 saw the publication of a work begun in 1704, mostly written by 1714, virtually complete by 1730, revised in 1734-36 : *Polite Conversation,* or, to give it the full title, *A Complete Collection of Genteel and Ingenious Conversation, According to the Most Polite Mode and Method Now Used at Court, and in the Best Companies of England. In Three Dialogues. By Simon Wagstaff, Esq.*

Inevitably associated with *Polite Conversation* is the *Hints towards an Essay on Conversation,* which, although unpublished until 1763, seems to have been written in or about the year 1710, for internal evidence shows it to be, in temper and style, related to the *Tatler* essay. Whereas the title and the Introduction to the three dialogues of *Polite Conversation* are brilliantly ironic, *An Essay on Conversation* is brilliantly sarcastic. But since the *Essay* is very much less important than the *Conversation,* one needs only to say that Swift is here no less 'concerned with the problem of maintaining the integrity of the mother tongue for the purposes of writing and conversation' (Herbert Davis) than he is in the *Tatler* essay, the *Proposal for Correcting the English Tongue,* the *Letter to a Young Clergyman;* that he describes and analyzes the bores and other spoil-sports, the 'menaces' of conversation, more appositely, more pertinently and forcibly, than anyone else has done either before or since his day; and that he attributes that degeneracy which affected the conversation of the period mainly to 'the Custom arisen, for some Years past, of excluding Women from any Share in our Society, farther than in Parties at Play, or Dancing, or in the

Pursuit of an Amour'. The *Essay on Conversation* is a delightful piece of work : and most of us could wish that it had grown into a fully developed study or treatise.

POLITE CONVERSATION

This work consists of 'An Introduction to the following Treatise' (a title no less ironic, no less mock-pompous, than the introduction itself) – running to perhaps ten thousand words – and, in three dialogues, 'A Compleat Collection of Genteel and Ingenious Conversation' – amounting to perhaps twenty thousand words.

Many of his friends and acquaintances, of his reviewers and readers, were bound to recognize the authorship, yet he used the pseudonym 'Simon Wagstaff, Esq.', which in itself betrayed him to those older members of the public who knew or guessed this to be a variation of the 'Isaac Bickerstaff, Esq.' who had made something of a stir in the literary and social circles of from thirty to twenty-seven years earlier : humorous elaborations of the literary surname *Staff*, a product of the fanciful and ingenious minds of Steele and Swift – 'the famous family of the Staffs of Staffordshire, whose genealogy was given in *The Tatler*, No. 11, for May 5, 1709' (Herbert Davis) – a surname that, according to Dr P. H. Reaney, *A Dictionary of British Surnames*, is recorded as early as 1177 and is 'used by Chaucer as a type of thinness or leanness'; but, by Swift, probably to imply a trustworthy support. Moreover, *bicker-* clearly alludes to the fact that in the various 'Bickerstaff' essays and papers he was being severely critical, and *wag-* to the equally evident fact that, as 'Wagstaff', he was being 'a merry droll' – as Samuel Johnson, only ten years after Swift's death, was to define *wag*.

The language of the dialogues very probably belongs to the reign of Queen Anne : 1702-1714. Their author may have made a few linguistic modifications, as he certainly made a few necessary historical alterations in order that the conversations should not suffer from the handicap of being 'dated'. As Professor Herbert Davis has judiciously remarked, 'The impression of the *Dialogues*, as a whole, is extraordinary timeless and Swift is entirely justified in his boast that

> my collection of discourse hath descended by
> tradition for at least an hundred years, without
> any change in the phraseology.

And we may well accept his statement that

> these polite questions, answers, repartees,
> replies, and rejoinders [had been collected] with
> infinite labour, and close application, during
> the space of thirty-six years.'

The timelessness does not extend to the slangy truncations (*incog, rep, fizz,* etc.) occurring towards the end of the first dialogue, nor yet perhaps to a very few of the catch-phrases; such exceptions merely strengthen the generalization.

The colloquial fluency and liveliness of the Dialogues are matched by the easy, good-humoured – but correct, not colloquial – style of the Introduction. The playfulness and good humour of the Introduction correspond to those of *An Essay on Conversation,* but we must not allow these agreeable qualities to blind us to the serious purpose of both : to scarify the vanity and the monopoly, the pedantry and desperate attempts to be witty, the ill-bred interruptions and the ill-mannered raillery and mockery, that disfigure so many conversations, especially when there are three or more interlocutors. Thus he prepares – almost conditions – us for that 'perfection of folly' which characterizes the dialogues themselves and which, indeed, invests them with a value all their own. Often we learn more from fools happily exhibiting their folly than from the wise expounding their usually too carefully expressed wisdom. The conscious is instructive; the subconscious, dazzling in the enlightenment it sheds and the damnations it divulges. It is precisely because the interlocutors speak without thinking, that they become real, and their conversation genuine and revelatory.

'The three Dialogues that make up the actual conversations all take place at Lord Smart's house in St James' Park, with the same small company at breakfast, at dinner, and afterwards at tea with the ladies; Sir John Linger, the Derbyshire squire, appears only in the Second Dialogue, as he joins them for a while at dinner. Nothing is spared us, from the opening greetings on the street to the final leave-takings – all the small-talk, witty remarks, repartees, common proverbs; we might well suppose that Swift had ransacked all the phrase-books and the collections of proverbs, and simply rearranged them in a continuous flow of conversation' : thus Professor Herbert Davis in his neat, perceptive summary. But, as Professor Davis himself observes, Swift may have done exactly what Simon Wagstaff said *he* did : jotted down in a note-book, as soon as ever he could, the conversations he had lately heard.

Two points, however, need to be emphasized. The very numerous disparates forming the conversations have been linked with immense skill; and if, as Professor James Sutherland once remarked to me, no conversation, if reported word for word, would – or could – contain, so closely packed, quite so many proverbs and catch-phrases as Swift crams into a single Dialogue, this fact does not lessen the validity and veracity of the three sustained dialogues. These dialogues are no more to be called 'set pieces' than the most life-like dialogues in comedies dealing with a contemporaneous scene, no matter at what period they were written; in the fact, they are rather less 'set', for manifestly they contain large chunks of conversation that bears every mark of having been recorded verbatim or, at worst, with the addition of that modicum of art which every dramatic or literary work requires : the pauses bridged, the hesitations either shortened or completely ignored, the *ahs* and *ers* and *ums* either reduced in number or merely intimated, the solecisms slurred over or otherwise mitigated, the sloppy syntax clarified, the anacolutha rendered less glaring, to particularize but a few of the means whereby even the most realistic of writers of dialogue 'improve on Nature'.

There was perhaps another reason why Swift crammed the Dialogues with proverbs, catch-phrases, colloquialisms, banalities : he may have wished – being a sensible man and a practised writer, he probably did wish – to keep the three conversations down to a reasonable length. Professor Dobrée, who adjudges the Introduction 'superb, and still valuable', finds the conversation 'amusingly readable, though we may think that it is here and there a little heavy, and that it goes on too long'. But only critics and reviewers can 'have it both ways' : writers must, according to their abilities, decide how best to tackle a difficult project. Swift, after all, was not trying to prove how witty he was, even though he could not hide that agreeable fact; he was aiming to provide 'a *compleat* collection of genteel and ingenious conversation' (the italics are mine) – not a mere sketch, much less a specimen, either of which might justly have been condemned as inadequate to his purpose. Saintsbury has put the case very justly when, in the introduction to his edition of *Polite Conversation*, he says that the work 'is never unequal; it never flags; it never forces the note. Nobody, if he likes it at all, can think it too long; nobody, however much he may like it, can fail to see that Swift was wise not to make it longer.'

The conversational styles of the five male participants are sharply distinguished, both individually, one from another, and generally, from those of the three women. The speech of Miss Notable is always distinct from that of Lady Smart or Lady Answerall. Occasionally, however, that of Lady Smart is insufficiently differentiated from that of Lady Answerall; yet on these few occasions we should, even without the stage directions, usually be able to guess which it is, from the fact that Lady Smart is the hostess. As G. A. Aitken has remarked, 'Miss Notable and Mr Neverout were described with special care; for they were intended to be patterns for all young bachelors and single ladies. Sir John Linger, the Derbyshire knight, was made to speak in his own rude dialect, to show what should be avoided.' Miss Notable is easily the most attractive character : and easily the best analysis of her character, with its naturalness and independence and self-respect, is that made by Saintsbury, who frankly confesses, 'I fell in love with her when I was about seventeen, I think; and from that day to this I have never wavered for one minute in my affection for her'. Like Saintsbury, the present editor also highly esteems Lord Smart, whose portrait has been silhouetted rather than formally painted. In his quiet way, he is, among the men, 'the pick of the bunch'. Clearly, too, the Colonel is something of a character. Tom Neverout is rather too brash and conceited; perhaps he felt that he had to assert himself.

Swift's Introduction could have stood alone. Had it done so, we should have the better appreciated its very great merits. Once again, George Saintsbury has delivered the final verdict. 'Although there are more magnificent and more terrible, more poignant and more whimsical examples of the marvellous Swiftian irony, I do not know that there is any more justly proportioned, more exquisitely modulated, more illustrative of that wonderful keeping' – congruity or harmony – 'which is the very essence and quiddity of the Dean's humour.'

Yet it does usher in the dialogues; which, in their turn, serve as a consummate foil. They, too, could perhaps have stood alone, but, had they done so, they would have lost their point; at least, their literary point.

Their linguistic point is quite another matter. This *Collection of Genteel Conversation* forms by far the best single record of polite English spoken at any given period, not merely up to and including that of Swift himself, but also, indeed, after him. By that apparently sweeping statement, I mean that there exists no other single literary work – for instance, a play, a novel, an autobiography – containing either material so rich and accurate or examples so numerous and apposite, a fluency and naturalness so smoothly and skilfully conveyed, an atmosphere so genuine, characters so true to life, as this record of literate English at the colloquial level. These conversations illustrate the spoken syntax and accidence, the spoken words and phrases, the current proverbs and catch-phrases, the greetings and farewells, the oaths and exclamations, the very tempo and spirit and tendencies, of the early eighteenth century : and, except to the nitwits and the half-wits, they are, in very large part, perfectly intelligible today. My commentary, therefore, is intended primarily to heighten and illuminate the role of Swift's contribution to the history and study of spoken English and, secondarily, to relate the spoken English of his day to that of the twentieth century. I am, in short, offering much less a super-imposition than a parallel – and a continuous means of comparison.

A COMPLETE

COLLECTION

Of GENTEEL and INGENIOUS

CONVERSATION,

According to the Most

Polite Mode and Method

Now USED

At COURT, and in the BEST COMPANIES of ENGLAND.

In THREE DIALOGUES.

By *SIMON WAGSTAFF*, Esq;

LONDON:

Printed for B. MOTTE, and C. BATHURST, at the *Middle Temple-Gate* in *Fleet-street.*

M.DCC.XXXVIII.

AN
INTRODUCTION
To the following
TREATISE

AS my Life hath been chiefly spent in consulting the Honour
and Welfare of my Country, for more than forty Years past;
not without answerable Success, if the World, and my
Friends, have not flattered me; so, there is no Point wherein I have
so much laboured, as that of improving, and polishing all Parts of
Conversation between Persons of Quality, whether they meet by
Accident or Invitation, at Meals, Tea, or Visits, Mornings, Noons,
or Evenings.

I HAVE passed, perhaps, more Time, than any other Man of my
Age and Country, in Visits, and Assemblies, where the polite
Persons, of both Sexes, distinguish themselves; and could not, with-
out much Grief observe, how frequently both Gentlemen, and
Ladies, are at a Loss for Questions, Answers, Replies, and Re-
joynders. However, my Concern was much abated, when I found,
that these Defects were not occasioned by any Want of Materials,
but because these Materials were not in every Hand. For Instance:
One Lady can give an Answer better than ask a Question. One
Gentleman is happy at a Reply; another excels in a Rejoynder:
One can revive a languishing Conversation, by a sudden surprizing
Sentence; another is more dextrous in seconding; a third can fill
the Gap with laughing or commending what hath been said. Thus,
fresh Hints may be started, and the Ball of Discourse kept up.

BUT alas, this is too seldom the Case, even in the most select
Companies. How often do we see at Court, at publick visiting Days,
or great Men's Levees, and other Places of general Meeting, that
the Conversation falls and drops to nothing, like a Fire without
supply of Fuel. This is what we all ought to lament; and against
this dangerous Evil, I take upon me to affirm, that I have in the
following Papers provided an infallible Remedy.

IT was in the Year 1695, and the Sixth of his late Majesty King
WILLIAM the Third, of ever glorious and immortal Memory, who

rescued three Kingdoms from Popery and Slavery; when being about the Age of six and thirty, my Judgment mature, of good Reputation in the World, and well acquainted with the best Families in Town; I determined to spend five Mornings, to dine four Times, pass three Afternoons, and six Evenings every Week, in the Houses of the most polite Families; of which I would confine my self to fifty; only changing as the Masters or Ladies died, or left the Town, or grew out of Vogue, or sunk in their Fortunes, or (which to me was of the highest Moment) became disaffected to the Government: Which Practice I have followed ever since, to this very Day; except, when I happened at any Time to be sick, or in[1] the Spleen[1] upon cloudy Weather; and except, when I entertained four of each Sex in my own Lodgings once a Month, by Way of Retaliation.

I always kept a large Table-Book[2] in my Pocket; and as soon as I left the Company, I immediately entred the choicest Expressions that passed during the Visit; which, returning home, I transcribed in a fair Hand, but somewhat enlarged; and had made the greatest Part of my Collection in twelve Years, but not digested into any Method: For, this I found was a Work of infinite Labour, and what required the nicest Judgment, and consequently could not be brought to any Degree of Perfection, in less than sixteen Years more: Herein, I resolved to exceed the Advice[3] of *Horace*,[3] a *Roman* Poet, (which I have read in Mr. *Creech*'s admirable Translation) that an Author should keep his Works nine Years in his Closet, before he ventured to publish them; and finding, that I still received some additional Flowers of Wit and Language, although in a very small Number, I determined to defer the Publication, to pursue my Design, and exhaust, if possible, the whole Subject, that I might present a compleat System to the World. For, I am convinced by long Experience, that the Criticks will be as severe as their old Envy against me can make them. I foresee they will object, that I have inserted many Answers and Replies, which are neither witty, humourous, polite, or authentick; and have omitted others, that would have been highly useful, as well as entertaining. But let them come to Particulars, and I will boldly engage to confute their Malice.

For these last six or seven Years, I have not been able to add above nine valuable Sentences to enrich my Collection: From whence I conclude, that what remains, will amount only to a trifle. However, if after the Publication of this Work, any Lady or Gentleman when they have read it, shall find the least Thing of Importance omitted, I desire they will please to supply my Defects, by communicating to me their Discoveries; and their Letters may be directed to *Simon Wagstaff*, Esq; at his Lodgings next Door to the *Glocester* Head in St. *James*'s Street, (paying the Postage)[3a] in return of which Favour, I shall make honourable mention of their Names in a short Preface to the second Edition.

IN the mean Time, I cannot but with some Pride, and much Pleasure, congratulate with my dear Country, which hath outdone all the Nations of *Europe*, in advancing the whole Art of Conversation, to the greatest Height it is capable of reaching. And therefore, being entirely convinced, that the Collection I now offer to the Publick, is full and compleat; I may at the same Time boldly affirm, that the whole Genius, Humour, Politeness, and Eloquence of *England*, are summed up in it. Nor, is the Treasure small, wherein are to be found, at least, a thousand shining Questions, Answers, Repartees, Replies, and Rejoynders, fitted to adorn every Kind of Discourse that an Assembly of *English* Ladies, and Gentlemen, met together for their mutual Entertainment can possibly want: especially when the several Flowers shall be set off and improved by the Speakers with every Circumstance of Preface and Circumlocution in proper Terms; and attended with Praise, Laughter, or Admiration. There is a natural involuntary Distortion of the Muscles, which is the anatomical Cause of Laughter: But there is another Cause of Laughter which Decency requires, and is the undoubted Mark of a good Taste, as well as of a polite obliging Behaviour; neither is this to be acquired without much Observation, long Practice, and a sound Judgment. I did therefore once intend, for the Ease of the Learner, to set down in all Parts of the following Dialogues, certain Marks, Asterisks, or Nota Bene's, (in *English*, Mark-well's) after most Questions, and every Reply or Answer; directing exactly the Moment when one, two, or all the Company are to laugh. But, having duly considered that this Expedient would too much enlarge the Bulk of the Volume, and consequently the Price; and likewise, that something ought to be left for ingenious Readers to find out: I have determined to leave the whole Affair, although of great Importance, to their own Discretion.

THE Reader must learn by all Means to distinguish between Proverbs, and those polite Speeches which beautify Conversation: For, as to the former, I utterly reject them out of all ingenious Discourse. I acknowledge indeed, that there may possibly be found in this Treatise a few Sayings among so great a Number of smart Turns of Wit and Humour as I have produced, which have a proverbial Air. However, I hope it will be considered, that even these were not originally Proverbs, but the genuine Productions of superior Wits, to embellish and support Conversation; from whence, with great Impropriety, as well as Plagiarism, (if you will forgive a hard Word) they have most injuriously been transferred into proverbial Maxims; and therefore, ought in Justice to be resumed out of vulgar Hands, to adorn the Drawing-Rooms of Princes, both Male and Female, the Levees of great Ministers, as well as the Toylet and Tea-Table of the Ladies.

I CAN faithfully assure the Reader, that there is not one single witty Phrase[4] in this whole Collection, which hath not received the Stamp and Approbation of at least one hundred Years; and, how much longer, it is hard to determine; he may therefore be secure to find them all genuine, sterling, and authentick.

BUT, before this elaborate Treatise can become of universal Use and Ornament to my native Country, two Points that will require Time and much Application, are absolutely necessary. For, first, whatever Person would aspire to be compleatly Witty, Smart, Humorous, and Polite; must by hard Labour be able to retain in his Memory every single Sentence contained in this Work; so as never to be once at a Loss in applying the right Answers, Questions, Repartees, and the like immediately, and without Study or Hesitation. And secondly, after a Lady or Gentleman hath so well overcome this Difficulty as to be never at a Loss upon any Emergency; the true Management of every Feature, and of almost every Limb is equally necessary; without which an infinite Number of Absurdities will inevitably ensue. For Instance; there is hardly a polite Sentence in the following Dialogues, which doth not absolutely require some peculiar graceful Motion in the Eyes, or Nose, or Mouth, or Forehead, or Chin; or suitable Toss of the Head, with certain Offices assigned to each Hand; and in Ladies, the whole Exercise[5] of the Fan,[5] fitted to the Energy of every Word they deliver: By no Means omitting the various Turns and Cadencies of the Voice, the Twistings, and Movements, and different Postures of the Body; the several Kinds and Gradations of Laughter, which the Ladies must daily practise by the Looking-Glass, and consult upon them with their Waiting-Maids.

MY Readers will soon observe what a great Compass of real and useful Knowledge this Science includes; wherein, although Nature

assisted by a Genius, may be very instrumental, yet a strong Memory
and constant Application, together with Example and Precept, will
be highly necessary. For these Reasons, I have often wished, that
certain Male and Female Instructors, perfectly versed in this Science,
would set up Schools for the Instruction of young Ladies and
Gentlemen therein. I remember about thirty Years ago, there was a
Bohemian[6] Woman, of that Species commonly known by the Name
of Gypsies, who came over hither from *France,* and generally
attended *Isaac*[6a] the Dancing-Master,[6a] when he was teaching his
Art to Misses of Quality; and while the young Ladies were thus
employed, the *Bohemian* standing at some Distance, but full in their
Sight, acted before them all proper Airs, and Heavings of the Head,
and Motions of the Hands, and Twistings of the Body; whereof
you may still observe the good Effects in several of our elder Ladies.
After the same Manner, it were much to be desired, that some
expert Gentlewomen, gone to Decay, would set up publick Schools,
wherein young Girls of Quality or great Fortunes, might first be
taught to repeat this following System of Conversation, which I
have been at so much Pains to compile; and then to adapt every
Feature of their Countenances, every Turn of their Hands, every
screwing of their Bodies, every Exercise of their Fans, to the Humour
of the Sentences they hear or deliver in Conversation. But above
all, to instruct them in every Species and Degree of Laughing, in
the proper Seasons at their own Wit, or that of the Company. And,
if the Sons of the Nobility and Gentry, instead of being sent to
common Schools, or put into the Hands of Tutors at Home, to learn
nothing but Words, were consigned to able Instructors in the same
Art; I cannot find what Use there could be of Books, except in the
Hands of those who are to make Learning their Trade; which is
below the Dignity of Persons born to Titles or Estates.

IT would be another infinite Advantage, that by cultivating this
Science, we should wholly avoid the Vexations and Impertinence of
Pedants; who affect to talk in a Language not to be understood;
and, whenever a polite Person offers accidentally to use any of their
Jargon-Terms,[7] have the Presumption to laugh at *us* for pronouncing those Words in a genteeler Manner : Whereas, I do here affirm,
that whenever any fine Gentleman or Lady condescends to let a
hard Word pass out of their Mouths, every Syllable is smoothed and
polished in the Passage; and, it is a true Mark of Politeness both
in Writing and Reading, to vary the Orthography as well as the
Sound, because we are infinitely better Judges of what will please

a distinguishing Ear, than those who call themselves Scholars, can possibly be; who consequently ought to correct their Books, and Manner of pronouncing by the Authority of our Example, from whose Lips they proceed with infinite more Beauty and Significancy.

BUT, in the mean Time, until so great, so useful, and so necessary a Design can be put in Execution, (which considering the good Disposition of our Country at present, I shall not despair of living to see) let me recommend the following Treatise, to be carried about as a Pocket Companion, by all Gentlemen and Ladies, when they are going to visit, or dine, or drink Tea; or, where they happen to pass the Evening without Cards; (as I have sometimes known it to be the Case, upon Disappointments, or Accidents unforeseen) desiring they would read their several Parts in their Chairs or Coaches, to prepare themselves for every Kind of Conversation, that can probably happen.

ALTHOUGH I have, in Justice to my Country, allowed the Genius of our People to excel that of any other Nation upon Earth; and have confirmed this Truth by an Argument not to be controuled, I mean, by producing so great a Number of witty Sentences in the ensuing Dialogues, all of undoubted Authority, as well as of our own Production; yet I must confess, at the same Time, that we are wholly indebted for them to our Ancestors; at least, for as long as my Memory reacheth, I do not recollect one new Phrase of Importance to have been added : Which Defect in us Moderns, I take to have been occasioned by the Introduction of Cant-Words,[8] in the Reign of King *Charles* the Second. And these have so often varied, that hardly one of them of above a Year's standing is now intelligible; nor any where to be found, excepting a small Number strowed here and there in the Comedies, and other fantastick Writings of that Age. The Honourable Colonel *James Graham*,[9] my old Friend and Companion, did likewise towards the End of the same Reign, invent a Set of Words and Phrases, which continued almost to the Time of his Death. But, as these Terms of Art were adapted only to Courts and Politicians, and extended little further than among his particular Acquaintance, (of whom I had the Honour to be one) they are now almost forgotten. Nor did the late D—— of R——,[10] and E—— of E——,[11] succeed better, although they proceeded no further than single Words; whereof, except *Bite*,[12] *Bamboozle*,[13] and one or two more, the whole Vocabulary is antiquated. The same Fate hath already attended those other Town Wits, who furnish us with a great Variety of new Terms, which are annually changed, and those of the last Season sunk in Oblivion. Of these, I was once favoured with a compleat List, by the Right Honourable the Lord and Lady H——,[14] with which I made a considerable Figure, one Summer, in the Country, but returning up to Town in Winter, and venturing to produce them again, I was partly hooted,[15] and partly not understood.

THE only Invention of late Years, which hath any Way contributed to advance Politeness in Discourse, is that of abbreviating,[16] or reducing Words of many Syllables into one, by lopping off the rest. This Refinement, having begun about the Time of the Revolution,[17] I had some Share in the Honour of promoting it; and I observe to my great Satisfaction, that it makes daily Advancements; and, I hope, in Time will raise our Language to the utmost Perfection: Although, I must confess, to avoid Obscurity, I have been very sparing of this Ornament in the following Dialogues.

BUT, as for Phrases invented to cultivate Conversation, I defy all the Clubs and Coffee-Houses in this Town, to invent a new one, equal in Wit, Humour, Smartness, or Politeness, to the very worst of my Set; which clearly shews, either that we are much degenerated, or that the whole Stock of Materials hath been already employed. I would willingly hope, as I do confidently believe, the latter: Because, having my self for several Months racked my Invention, if possible, to enrich this Treasury with some Additions of my own, (which, however, should have been printed in a different Character, that I might not be charged with imposing upon the Publick) and having shewn them to some judicious Friends, they dealt very sincerely with me; all unanimously agreeing, that mine were infinitely below the true old Helps to Discourse, drawn up in my present Collection, and confirmed their Opinion with Reasons by which I was perfectly convinced, as well as ashamed of my great Presumption.

BUT, I lately met a much stronger Argument to confirm me in the same Sentiments. For, as the great Bishop *Burnet*,[18] of *Salisbury*, informs us, in the Preface to his admirable History of his own Times; that he intended to employ himself in polishing it every Day of his Life, (and, indeed in its Kind, it is almost equally polished with this Work of mine) so, it hath been my constant Business, for some Years past, to examine with the utmost Strictness, whether I could possibly find the smallest Lapse in Style, or Propriety through my whole Collection, that in Emulation with the Bishop I might send it abroad, as the most finished Piece of the Age. It happened one Day, as I was dining in good Company of both Sexes, and watching, according to my Custom, for new Materials, wherewith to fill my Pocket Book, I succeeded well enough, until after Dinner, when the Ladies retired to their Tea, and left us over a Bottle of Wine. But, I found we were not able to furnish any more Materials that were worth the Pains of transcribing. For, the Discourse of the Company was all degenerated into smart Sayings of their own Invention, and not of the true old Standard; so that, in absolute Despair, I withdrew, and went to attend the Ladies at their Tea. From whence, I did then conclude, and still continue to believe, either that Wine doth not inspire Politeness, or that our Sex is not able to support it without the Company of Women, who never fail to lead us into the right Way, and there to keep us.

IT much encreaseth the Value of these Apophthegms, that unto them we owe the Continuance of our Language for at least an hundred Years; neither is this to be wondered at: Because, indeed, besides the Smartness of the Wit, and Fineness of the Raillery, such is the Propriety and Energy of Expression in them all, that they never can be changed but to Disadvantage, except in the Circumstance of using Abbreviations, which, however, I do not despair, in due Time, to see introduced, having already met them in some of the choice Companies in Town.

ALTHOUGH this Work be calculated for all Persons of Quality and Fortune, of both Sexes, yet the Reader may perceive, that my particular View was to the Officers of the Army, the Gentlemen of the Inns of Courts, and of both the Universities; to all Courtiers, Male and Female; but, principally to the Maids of Honour, of whom I have been personally acquainted with two and twenty Setts, all excelling in this noble Endowment; until some Years past, I know not how, they came to degenerate into selling of Bargains,[19] and Free-Thinking,[20] not, that I am against either of these Entertainments at proper Seasons, in Complyance with Company, who may Want a Taste for more exalted Discourse, whose Memories may be short; who are too young to be perfect in their Lessons: Or, (although it be hard to conceive) who have no Inclination to read and learn my Instructions. Besides, I confess, there is a strong Temptation for Court Ladies to fall into the two Amusements above-mentioned, that they may avoid the Censure of affecting Singularity, against the general Current and Fashion of all about them: But however, no Man will pretend to affirm, that either Bargains or Blasphemy,[21] which are the principal Ornaments of

Free-Thinking, are so good a Fund of polite Discourse, as what is to be met with in my Collection. For, as to Bargains; few of them seem to be excellent in their Kind, and have not much Variety, because they all terminate in one single Point; and, to multiply them would require more Invention than People have to spare. And, as to Blasphemy or Free-Thinking, I have known some scrupulous Persons of both Sexes, who, by a prejudiced Education, are afraid of Sprights.[22] I must however except the Maids of Honour, who have been fully convinced, by a famous Court-Chaplain,[23] that there is no such Place as Hell.

I CANNOT indeed, controvert the Lawfulness of Free-Thinking, because it hath been universally allowed, that Thought is free. But however, although it may afford a large Field of Matter, yet, in my poor Opinion, it seems to contain very little, either of Wit or Humour; because, it hath not been ancient enough among us, to furnish established authentick Expressions; I mean such as must receive a Sanction from the polite World, before their Authority can be allowed; neither, was the Art of Blasphemy or Free-Thinking invented by the Court, or by Persons of great Quality, who properly speaking, were Patrons rather than Inventors of it, but first brought in by the Fanatick Faction,[24] towards the End of their Power; and, after the Restoration, carried to *Whitehall* by the converted Rumpers,[25] with very good Reason; because, they knew, that King *Charles* the Second, from a wrong Education, occasioned by the Troubles of his Father, had Time enough to observe, that Fanatick Enthusiasm[26] directly led to Atheism; which agreed with the dissolute Inclinations of his Youth: And, perhaps these Principles were farther cultivated in him by the *French* Huguenots,[27] who have been often charged for spreading them among us: However, I cannot see where the Necessity lies of introducing new and foreign Topicks for Conversation, while we have so plentiful a Stock of our own Growth.

I HAVE likewise, for some Reasons of equal Weight, been very sparing in Double-entendres,[28] because, they often put Ladies upon affected Constraints,[29] and affected Ignorance. In short, they break, or very much entangle the Thread of Discourse; neither am I Master of any Rules to settle the disconcerted Countenances of the Females in such a Juncture: I can therefore only allow Innuendoes of this Kind to be delivered in Whispers, and only to young Ladies under Twenty, who being in Honour obliged to blush, it may produce a new Subject for Discourse.

PERHAPS the Criticks may accuse me of a Defect in my following System of polite Conversation; that there is one great Ornament of Discourse, whereof I have not produced a single Example; which, indeed, I purposely omitted, for some Reasons, that I shall immediately offer; and, if those Reasons, will not satisfy the Male Part of my gentle Readers; the Defect may be supplied, in some Manner, by an Appendix to the Second Edition: Which Appendix shall be printed by itself, and sold for Six-pence stitched, and with a Marble Cover; that my Readers may have no Occasion to complain of being defrauded: The Defect I mean, is, my not having inserted into the Body of my Book, all the Oaths[30] now most in Fashion for embellishing Discourse; especially, since it could give no Offence to the Clergy, who are seldom, or never admitted to these polite Assemblies. And, it must be allowed, that Oaths well chosen, are not only very useful Expletives[31] to Matter, but great Ornaments of Style.

WHAT I shall here offer in my own Defence, upon this important Article, will, I hope, be some Extenuation of my Fault. First, I reasoned with my self, that a just Collection of Oaths, repeated as often as the Fashion requires, must have enlarged this Volume, at least to double the Bulk; whereby, it would not only double the Charge, but likewise make the Volume less commodious for Pocket Carriage. Secondly, I have been assured by some judicious Friends, that themselves have known certain Ladies to take Offence (whether seriously or no) at too great a Profusion of Cursing and Swearing; even, when that Kind of Ornament was not improperly introduced: Which, I confess, did startle me not a little; having never observed the like, in the Compass of my own Female Acquaintance, at least for twenty Years past. However, I was forced to submit to wiser Judgments than my own. Thirdly, as this most useful Treatise is calculated for all future Times; I considered, in this Maturity of my Age, how great a Variety of Oaths I have heard, since I began to study the World, and to know Men and Manners. And here, I found it to be true, what I have read in an ancient Poet:[32]

'For, nowadays, Men change their Oaths,
'As often as they change their Cloaths.'

IN short, Oaths are the Children of Fashion; they are, in some Sense, almost Annuals,[33] like what I observed before, of Cant-words; and I my self, can remember about forty different Setts. The old Stock-oaths, I am confident, do not amount to above forty-five, or fifty at most; but, the Way of mingling and compounding them, is almost as various, as that of the Alphabet. Sir *John Perrot*[34] was the first Man of Quality, whom I find upon Record, to have sworn by G——'s W——.[35] He lived in the Reign of Queen *Elizabeth*, and was supposed to have been a natural Son of *Harry* VIII. who might also have probably been his Instructor. This Oath, indeed, still continues, and is a Stock-oath to this Day; so do several others, that have kept their primitive natural Simplicity: But, infinitely the greater Number hath been so frequently changed, and dislocated, that if the Inventors were now alive, they could hardly understand them.

Upon these Considerations, I began to apprehend, that if I should insert all the Oaths as now current; my Book would be out of Vogue with the first Change of Fashion, and grow useless as an old Dictionary. Whereas, the Case is quite otherwise with my Collection of polite Discourse; which, as I before observed, hath descended by Tradition, for at least an hundred Years, without any Change in the Phraseology. I therefore determined with my self, to leave out the whole System of Swearing; because, both the Male and Female Oaths are all perfectly well known and distinguished; new Ones are easily learnt, and with a moderate Share of Discretion, may be properly applyed on every fit Occasion. However, I must here upon this Article of Swearing, most earnestly recommend to my Readers, that they would please a little to study Variety. For, it is the Opinion of our most refined Swearers, that the same Oath or Curse, cannot, consistent with true Politeness, be repeated above nine Times, in the same Company, by the same Person, and at one Sitting.

I am far from desiring, or expecting, that all the polite and ingenious Speeches contained in this Work, should in the general Conversation between Ladies and Gentlemen, come in so quick and so close, as I have here delivered them. By no Means: On the contrary, they ought to be husbanded better, and spread much thinner. Nor, do I make the least Question, but that by a discreet, thrifty Management, they may serve for the Entertainment of a whole Year; to any Person who doth not make too long, or too frequent Visits in the same Family. The Flowers of Wit, Fancy, Wisdom, Humour, and Politeness, scattered in this Volume, amount to one[36] thousand, seventy and four.[36] Allowing then to every Gentleman and Lady thirty visiting Families, (not insisting upon Fractions) there will want but little of an hundred polite Questions,

Answers, Replies, Rejoinders, Repartees, and Remarks, to be daily delivered, fresh in every Company, for twelve solar Months; and, even this, is a higher Pitch of Delicacy than the World insists on, or, hath reason to expect. But, I am altogether for exalting this Science to its utmost Perfection.

IT may be objected, that the Publication of my Book, may, in a long Course of Time, prostitute this noble Art to mean and vulgar People. But, I answer; that it is not so easily acquired, as a few ignorant Pretenders may imagine. A Footman can swear; but he cannot swear like a Lord. He can swear as often: But, can he swear with equal Delicacy, Propriety, and Judgment? No certainly; unless he be a Lad of superior Parts, of good Memory, a diligent Observer, one who hath a skilful Ear, some Knowledge in Musick, and an exact Taste; which hardly falls to the Share of one in a thousand among that Fraternity, in as high Favour as they now stand with their Ladies; neither, perhaps hath one Footman in six, so fine a Genius, as to relish and apply those exalted Sentences comprised in this Volume, which I offer to the World: It is true, I cannot see that the same ill Consequences would follow from the Waiting-woman, who, if she hath been bred to read Romances,[37] may have some small subaltern or second-hand Politeness; and, if she constantly attends the Tea, and be a good Listner, may, in some Years, make a tolerable Figure; which, will serve perhaps, to draw in the young Chaplain, or the old Steward. But, alas! after all, how can she acquire, those hundreds of Graces and Motions, and Airs, the whole military Management of the Fan, the Contorsions of every muscular Motion in the Face; the risings and fallings; the quickness, and slackness of the Voice, with the several Tones and Cadences; the proper Junctures of smiling and frowning; how often, and how loud to laugh; when to jibe and when to flout; with all the other Branches of Doctrine and Discipline above recited. I am therefore, not under the least Apprehension, that this Art will be ever in Danger of falling into common Hands, which requires so much Time, Study, Practice, and Genius, before it arrives to Perfection: And therefore, I must repeat my Proposal for erecting publick Schools, provided with the best and ablest Masters and Mistresses, at the Charge of the Nation.

I HAVE drawn this Work into the Form of a Dialogue, after the Pattern of other famous Writers in History, Law, Politicks, and most Arts and Sciences, and I hope it will have the same Success: For, who can contest it to be of greater Consequence to the Happiness of these Kingdoms, than all human *Knowledge* put together. Dialogue is held the best Method of inculcating any Part of Knowledge: And, as I am confident, that publick Schools will soon be founded for teaching Wit and Politeness, after my Scheme, to young People of Quality and Fortune; so I have determined, next Sessions, to deliver a Petition to the House of Lords, for an Act of Parliament to establish my Book, as the standard Grammar,[38] in all the principal Cities of both Kingdoms, where this Art is to be taught, by able Masters, who are to be approved and recommended by me; which is no more than *Lilly*[39] obtained, only for teaching Words in a Language wholly useless: Neither, shall I be so far wanting to my self, as not to desire a Patent, granted of Course to all useful Projectors,[40] I mean, that I may have the sole Profit of giving a Licence to every such School, to read my Grammar for fourteen Years.

THE Reader cannot but observe, what Pains I have been at in polishing the Style of my Book to the greatest Exactness: Nor, have I been less diligent in refining the Orthography,[41] by spelling the Words in the very same Manner that they are pronounced. Wherein I follow the chief Patterns of Politeness, at Court, at Levees, at Assemblies, at Play-houses, at the prime visiting Places, by young Templers, and by Gentlemen Commoners of both Universities, who have lived, at least, a Twelve-month in Town, and kept the best Company: Of these Spellings, the Publick will meet with many Examples, in the following Book: For Instance,[42] can't, hav'n't, sha'n't, didn't, coodn't, woodn't, isn't, e'n't;[42] with many more. Besides several Words, which Scholars pretend, are derived from *Greek* and *Latin*; but now pared into a polite Sound, by Ladies, Officers of the Army, Courtiers and Templers; such as Jommetry[43] for Geometry, Verdi for Verdict, Lard for Lord, Larnin[43] for Learning; together with some Abbreviations exquisitely refined: As, Pozz[44] for Positively, Mobb[45] for Mobile, Phizz[46] for Physiognomy, Rep[47] for Reputation, Plenipo[48] for Plenipotentiary, Incog[49] for Incognito, Hipps,[50] or Hippo[50] for Hypocondriacks, Bam[51] for Bamboozle,[52] and Bamboozle for God knows what; whereby much Time is saved, and the high Road to Conversation, cut short by many a Mile.

I HAVE, as it will be apparent, laboured very much, and I hope with Felicity enough, to make every Character in the Dialogue, agreeable with itself; to a Degree, that whenever any judicious Person shall read my Book aloud for the Entertainment and Instruction of a select Company, he need not so much as name the particular Speakers; because, all the Persons throughout the several Subjects of Conversation, strictly observe a different Manner peculiar to their Characters, which are of different Kinds; but, this I leave entirely to the prudent and impartial Reader's Discernment.

PERHAPS, the very Manner of introducing the several Points of Wit and Humour, may not be less entertaining and instructing than the Matter itself: In the latter, I can pretend to little Merit; because, it entirely depends upon Memory, and the Happiness of having kept polite Company. But, the Art of contriving that those Speeches should be introduced naturally, as the most proper Sentiments to be delivered upon so great a Variety of Subjects; I take to be a Talent somewhat uncommon, and a Labour that few People could hope to succeed in; unless, they had a Genius particularly turned that Way, added to a sincere disinterested Love of the Publick.

ALTHOUGH, every curious Question, smart Answer, and witty Reply, be little known to many People; yet, there is not one single Sentence in the whole Collection, for which I cannot bring most authentick Vouchers, whenever I shall be called: And, even for some Expressions, which to a few nicer Ears, may perhaps appear somewhat gross, I can produce the Stamp of Authority from Courts, Chocolate-houses,[53] Theatres, Assemblies, Drawing-rooms, Levees, Card-meetings, Balls, and Masquerades; from Persons of both Sexes, and of the highest Titles next to Royal. However, to say the Truth, I have been very sparing in my Quotations of such Sentiments that seem to be over free; because, when I began my Collection, such kind of Converse was almost in its Infancy, until it was taken into the Protection of my honoured Patronesses at Court; by whose Countenance and Sanction, it hath become a choice Flower, in the Nosegay of Wit and Politeness.

SOME will, perhaps, object, that when I bring my Company to Dinner, I mention too great a Variety of Dishes, not always consistent with the Art of Cookery, or proper for the Season of the Year; and part of the first Course mingled with the Second; besides a Failure in Politeness, by introducing Black-pudding[54] to a Lord's Table, and at a great Entertainment: But, if I had omitted the Black-pudding, I desire to know, what would have become of that exquisite Reason given by Miss *Notable* for not eating it. The World perhaps might have lost it for ever, and I should have been justly answerable for having left it out of my Collection. I therefore cannot but hope, that such Hypercritical Readers, will please to consider, my Business was to make so full and compleat a Body of refined Sayings, as compact as I could; only taking Care, to produce them in the most natural and probable Manner, in order to allure my Readers into the very Substance and Marrow of this most admirable and necessary Art.

I AM heartily sorry, and was much disappointed to find; that so universal and polite an Entertainment as Cards, hath hitherto contributed very little to the Enlargement of my Work. I have sate by many hundred Times with the utmost Vigilance, and my Table-Book ready, without being able in eight Hours, to gather Matter for one single Phrase in my Book. But this, I think, may be easily accounted for, by the Turbulence and Jostling of Passions upon the various and surprizing Turns, Incidents, Revolutions, and Events, of good and evil Fortune, that arrive in the Course of a long Evening at Play; the Mind being wholly taken up, and the Consequences of Non-Attention so fatal. Play is supported upon the two great Pillars of Deliberation and Action. The Terms of Art are few, prescribed by Law and Custom; no Time allowed for Digressions or Tryals of Wit. *Quadrille*[55] in particular, bears some Resemblance to a State of Nature, which we are told,[55a] is a State of War, wherein every Woman is against every Woman: The Unions short, inconstant, and soon broke; the League made this Minute, without knowing the Allye; and dissolved in the next. Thus, at the Game of *Quadrille,* Female Brains are always employed in Stratagem, or their Hands in Action.

NEITHER can I find, that our Art hath gained much by the happy Revival of masquerading[56] among us: The whole Dialogue in these Meetings, being summed up in one sprightly (I confess, but) single Question; and as sprightly an Answer. Do you know me? Yes, I do. And, Do you know me? Yes, I do. For this Reason, I did not think it proper, to give my Readers the Trouble of introducing a Masquerade,[56] meerly for the Sake of a single Question, and a single Answer. Especially, when to perform this in a proper Manner, I must have brought in a hundred Persons together of both Sexes, dressed in fantastick Habits for one Minute, and dismissed them the next. Neither is it reasonable to conceive, that our Science can be much improved by Masquerades, where the Wit of both Sexes is altogether taken up in contriving singular and humoursome Disguises; and their Thoughts entirely employed in bringing Intrigues, and Assignations of Gallantry to an happy Conclusion.

THE judicious Reader will readily discover, that I make Miss *Notable,* my Heroin; and Mr. *Thomas Neverout,* my Hero: I have laboured both their Characters with my utmost Ability. It is into their mouths that I have put the Liveliest Questions, Answers, Repartees, and Rejoynders; because, my Design was to propose them both as Patterns for all young Bachelors, and single Ladies to copy after. By which, I hope, very soon, to see polite Conversation flourish between both Sexes, in a more consummate Degree of Perfection than these Kingdoms have yet ever known.

I HAVE drawn some Lines of Sir *John Linger*'s Character, the *Derbyshire* Knight, on Purpose to place it in Counterview, or Contrast, with that of the other Company. Wherein, I can assure the Reader, that I intended not the least Reflection upon *Derby-shire,* the Place of my Nativity. But, my Intention was only to shew the Misfortune of those Persons, who have the Disadvantage to be bred out of the Circle of Politeness, whereof I take the present Limits, to extend no further than *London,* and ten Miles round, although others are pleased to confine it within the Bills of Mortality. If you compare the Discourses of my Gentlemen and Ladies with those of Sir *John*; you will hardly conceive him to have been bred in the same Climate, or under the same Laws, Language, Religion, or Government: And, accordingly I have introduced him speaking in his own rude Dialect,[57] for no other Reason than to teach my Scholars how to avoid it.

THE curious Reader will observe, that where Conversation appears in Danger to flag; which, in some Places, I have artfully contrived; I took Care to invent some sudden Question, or Turn of Wit to revive it. Such as these that follow. What? I think here is a silent Meeting. Come Madam, a[58] Penny for your Thought;[58] with several others of the like Sort.

I HAVE rejected all Provincial, or Country Turns of Wit, and Fancy, because I am acquainted with a very few; but indeed, chiefly, because I found them so very much inferior to those at Court, especially among the Gentlemen Ushers, the Ladies of the Bed-Chamber, and the Maids of Honour. I must also add the hither End of our noble Metropolis.

WHEN this happy Art of polite conversing, shall be thoroughly improved; good Company will be no longer pestered with dull dry tedious Story-tellers, or brangling Disputers. For, a right Scholar of either Sex, in our Science, will perpetually interrupt them with some sudden surprizing Piece of Wit, that shall engage all the Company in a loud Laugh; and, if after a Pause, the grave Companion resumes his Thread, in the following Manner; well;[59] but, to go on with my Story;[59] new Interruptions come from the Left and Right, until he be forced to give over.

I HAVE likewise made some few Essays, towards selling of Bargains, as well for instructing those who delight in that Accomplishment, as in Compliance with my Female Friends at Court. However, I have transgressed a little in this Point, by doing it in a Manner somewhat more reserved, than as it is now practised at St. *James*'s.[60] At the same Time, I can hardly allow this Accomplishment to pass properly for a Branch of that perfect polite Conversation, which makes the constituent Subject of my Treatise; and, for this, I have already given my Reasons. I have, likewise, for further Caution, left a Blank in the critical Point of each Bargain, which, the sagacious Reader may fill up in his own Mind.

As to my self; I am proud to own, that except some Smattering in the *French*, I am, what the Pedants, and Scholars call, a Man wholly illiterate; that is to say, unlearned. But, as to my own Language, I shall not readily yield to many Persons; I have read most of the Plays, and all the Miscellany Poems that have been published for twenty Years past. I have read Mr *Thomas Brown*'s[61] Works entire, and had the Honour to be his intimate Friend, who was universally allowed to be the greatest Genius of his Age. Upon what Foot I stand, with the present chief reigning Wits, their Verses recommendatory, which they have commanded me to prefix before my Book, will be more than a thousand Witnesses. I am, and have been likewise, particularly acquainted with Mr. *Charles Gildon*,[62] Mr. *Ward*,[63] Mr. *Dennis*,[64] that admirable Critick, and Poet; and several others. Each of these eminent Persons, (I mean those who are still alive) have done me the Honour to read this Production, five Times over, with the strictest Eye of friendly Severity; and proposed some, although very few Amendments, which, I gratefully accepted; and, do here publickly return my Acknowledgment for so singular a Favour. And, I cannot conceal, without Ingratitude, the great Assistance I have received from those two illustrious Writers Mr. *Ozel*,[65] and Captain *Stevens*.[66] These, and some others, of distinguished Eminency, in whose Company I have passed so many agreeable Hours; as they have been the great Refiners of our Language, so, it hath been my chief Ambition to imitate them. Let the *Popes*,[67] the *Gays*, the *Arbuthnots*, the *Youngs*,[67] and the rest of that snarling Brood, burst with Envy at the Praises we receive from the Court, and Kingdom. But, to return from this Digression.

THE Reader will find, that the following Collection of polite

Expressions, will easily incorporate with all Subjects of genteel and fashionable Life. Those which are proper for Morning Tea, will be equally useful at the same Entertainment in the Afternoon, even in the same Company, only by shifting the several Questions, Answers, and Replies, into different Hands; and, such as are adapted to Meals, will indifferently serve for Dinners, or Suppers, only distinguishing between Day-light and Candle-Light. By this Method, no diligent Person of a tolerable Memory, can ever be at a Loss.

IT hath been my constant Opinion, that every Man who is intrusted by Nature, with any useful Talent of the Mind, is bound by all the Tyes of Honour; and, that Justice which we all owe our Country, to propose to himself some one illustrious Action to be performed in his Life, for the publick Emolument: And, I freely confess, that so grand, so important an Enterprize as I have undertaken, and executed to the best of my Power, well deserved a much abler Hand, as well as a liberal Encouragement from the Crown. However, I am bound so far to acquit my self, as to declare, that I have often, and most earnestly intreated several of my above-named Friends, universally allowed to be of the first Rank in Wit and Politeness, that they would undertake a Work so honourable to themselves, and so beneficial to the Kingdom: But, so great was their Modesty, that they all thought fit to excuse themselves, and impose the Task on me; yet, in so obliging a Manner, and attended with such Compliments, on my poor Qualifications, that I dare not repeat. And, at last, their Intreaties, or rather, their Commands, added to that inviolable Love I bear to the Land of my Nativity, prevailed upon me to engage in so bold an Attempt.

I MAY venture to affirm, without the least Violation of Modesty, that there is no Man now alive, who hath by many Degrees, so just Pretensions as my self, to the highest Encouragement from the Crown, the Parliament, and the Ministry, towards bringing this Work to its due Perfection. I have been assured, that several great Heroes of Antiquity, were worshipped as Gods, upon the Merit of having civilized a fierce and barbarous People. It is manifest, I could have no other Intentions; and, I dare appeal to my very Enemies, if such a Treatise as mine, had been published some Years ago, and with as much Success, as I am confident this will meet; I mean, by turning the Thoughts of the whole Nobility, and Gentry, to the Study and Practice of polite Conversation; whether such mean, stupid Writers, as the *Craftsman*,[68] and his Abettors, could have been able to corrupt the Principles of so many hundred thousand Subjects, as to the Shame and Grief of every whiggish, loyal, true Protestant Heart, it is too manifest they have done. For, I desire the honest, judicious Reader, to make one Remark; that, after I have exhausted the whole * in sickly Pay-Day[69] (if I may so call it) of Politeness and Refinement, and faithfully digested it into the following Dialogues, there cannot be found one Expression relating to Politicks: That the Ministry is never mentioned, nor the Word *King,* above twice or thrice; and then, only to the Honour of Majesty. So very cautious were our wiser Ancestors, in forming Rules for Conversation, as never to give Offence to crowned Heads, nor interfere with Party Disputes in the State. And indeed, although there seem to be a close Resemblance between the two Words, *Politeness,* and *Politicks;* yet no Ideas are more inconsistent in their Natures. However, to avoid all Appearance of Disaffection, I have taken Care to enforce Loyalty, by an invincible Argument, drawn from the Fountain of this noble Science, in the following short Terms, that ought to be writ in Gold, MUST, IS FOR THE KING.[70] Which uncontroulable[71] Maxim, I took particular Care of introducing in the first Page of my Book; thereby, to instil only the best Protestant loyal Notions into the Minds of my Readers. Neither is it meerly my own private Opinion, that Politeness is the firmest Foundation upon which Loyalty can be supported: For, thus happily sings the never-to-be-too-much-admired †Lord *H——*,[72] in his truly sublime Poem, called *Loyalty defined.*[72]

> *Who's not polite, for the Pretender, is;*
> *A Jacobite, I know him by his Phizz,*

IN the like Manner, the divine Mr. *Tibbalds,* or *Theobalds,*[73] in one of his Birth-day Poems.

> *I am no Scollard, but I am polite,*
> *Therefore be sure, I am no Jacobite.*

HEAR likewise, to the same Purpose, that great Master of the poetick Quire, our most illustrious Laureat, Mr. *Colly Cibber.*[74]

> *Who in his Talk, can't speak a polite Thing,*
> *Will never loyal be, to George our King.*

I COULD produce many more shining Passages out of our

---

* *This Word is spelt by Latinists* Encyclopædia: *But, the judicious Author, wisely prefers the polite Reading before the Pedantick.*

† *It is erroneously printed in the* London *Edition,* Mr. Stephen Duck.

principal Poets of both Sexes, to confirm this momentous Truth. From whence, I think it may be fairly concluded, that whoever can most contribute towards propagating the Science contained in the following Sheets, through the Kingdoms of *Great Britain* and *Ireland,* may justly demand all the Favour that the wisest Court, and most judicious Senate, are able to confer, on the most deserving Subject. I leave the Application to my Readers.

THIS is the Work, which I have been so hardy to attempt, and without the least mercenary View. Neither, do I doubt of succeeding, to my full Wish, except among the Tories and their Abettors; who being all Jacobites, and consequently Papists in their Hearts, may perhaps, resolve not to read my Book; chusing, from a Want of true Taste, or by strong Affectation, rather to deny themselves the Pleasure and Honour of shining in polite Company, among the principal Genius's of both Sexes throughout the Kingdom, than adorn their Minds with this noble Art; and probably apprehending (as I confess, nothing is more likely to happen) that a true Spirit of Loyalty to the Protestant Succession should steal in along with it.

IF my favourable and gentle Readers could possibly conceive the perpetual Watchings, the numberless Toyls, the frequent Risings in the Night, to set down several ingenious Sentences, that I suddenly, or accidentally recollected; and which, without my utmost Vigilance, had been irrecoverably lost for ever: If they would consider, with what incredible Diligence, I daily, and nightly attended, at those Houses where Persons of both Sexes, and of the most distinguished Merit used to meet, and display their Talents: With what Attention I listned to all their Discourses, the better to retain them in my Memory; and then, at proper Seasons withdrew unobserved, to enter them in my Table-Book, while the Company little suspected what a noble Work I had then in Embrio:[75] I say, if all this were known to the World, I think it would be no great Presumption in me to expect at a proper Juncture, the publick Thanks of both Houses of Parliament, for the Service and Honour I have done to the whole Nation, by my single Pen.

ALTHOUGH I have never been once charged with the least Tincture of Vanity, the Reader will, I hope, give me Leave to put an easy Question. What is become of all the King of *Sweden*'s Victories? Where are the Fruits of them at this Day? Or, of what Benefit will they be to Posterity? Were not many of his greatest Actions owing, at least, in Part, to Fortune? Were not all of them owing to the Valour of his Troops, as much as to his own Conduct?

Could he have conquered the *Polish* King, or the *Czar of Muscovy*,[76] with his single Arm? Far be it from me, to envy or lessen the Fame he hath acquired: But, at the same Time, I will venture to say, without Breach of Modesty, that I, who have alone, with this Right Hand, subdued Barbarism, Rudeness, and Rusticity; who have established, and fixed for ever, the whole System of all true Politeness, and Refinement in Conversation; should think my self most inhumanly treated by my Countrymen, and would accordingly resent it as the highest Indignity, to be put upon the Level, in Point of Fame, in after Ages, with *Charles*[77] XII. late King of Sweden.[77]

AND yet, so incurable is the Love of Detraction, perhaps, beyond what the charitable Reader will easily believe, that I have been assured by more than one credible Person, how some of my Enemies have industriously whispered about, that one *Isaac Newton*,[78] an Instrument-Maker, formerly living near *Leicester* Fields, and afterwards a Workman in the Mint, at the Tower, might possibly pretend to vye with me for Fame in future Times. The Man, it seems, was knighted for making Sun-Dyals better than others of his Trade, and was thought to be a Conjurer, because he knew how to draw Lines and Circles upon a Slate, which no Body could understand. But, adieu to all noble Attempts for endless Renown, if the Ghost of an obscure Mechanick,[79] shall be raised up, to enter into Competition with me, only for his Skill in making Pot-hooks and Hangers, with a Pencil; which many thousand accomplished Gentlemen and Ladies can perform as well, with a Pen and Ink, upon a Piece of Paper, and in a Manner as little intelligible as those of Sir *Isaac*.

MY most ingenious Friend already mentioned, Mr *Colly Cibber*, who doth so much Honour to the Laurel Crown he deservedly wears (as he hath often done to many Imperial Diadems placed on his Head) was pleased to tell me, that if my Treatise were shaped into a Comedy, the Representation performed to Advantage on our Theatre, might very much contribute to the spreading of Polite Conversation among all Persons of Distinction through the whole Kingdom. I own, the Thought was ingenious, and my Friend's Intention good: But, I cannot agree to his Proposal. For, Mr. *Cibber* himself, allowed, that the Subjects handled in my Work being so numerous, and extensive, it would be absolutely impossible for one, two, or even six Comedies to contain them. From whence it will follow, that many admirable and essential Rules for Polite Conversation must be omitted. And here, let me do Justice to my Friend Mr. *Tibbalds*, who plainly confessed before Mr. *Cibber* himself, that such a Project, as it would be a great Diminution to my Honour, so it would intolerably mangle my Scheme, and thereby destroy the principal End at which I aimed; to form a compleat Body, or System, of this most useful Science in all its Parts. And therefore Mr. *Tibbalds,* whose Judgment was never disputed, chose rather to fall in with my Proposal mentioned before, of erecting publick Schools, and Seminaries, all over the Kingdom, to instruct the young People, of both Sexes, in this Art, according to my Rules, and in the Method that I have laid down.

I SHALL conclude this long, but necessary Introduction, with a Request, or, indeed, rather, a just and reasonable Demand from all Lords, Ladies, and Gentlemen, that, while they are entertaining and improving each other with those polite Questions, Answers,[80] Repartees, Replies, and Rejoynders,[80] which I have, with infinite Labour, and close Application, during the Space of thirty-six Years been collecting for their Service and Improvement, they shall, as an Instance of Gratitude, on every proper Occasion, quote my Name, after this, or the like Manner: *Madam, as our Master* Wagstaff *says. My Lord, as our Friend* Wagstaff *hath it.* I do likewise expect, that all my Pupils shall drink my Health every Day at Dinner and Supper, during my Life; and that they, or their Posterity, shall continue the same Ceremony, to my *not inglorious Memory,*[81] after my Decease, for ever.

NOTES ON SWIFT'S INTRODUCTION

1, 1, in the Spleen. Very much depressed or very morose. *Spleen*, gloominess, excessive dejection, arose in the 1660's; earlier, it had denoted melancholy, from the spleen being regarded as the seat of melancholy. See especially Matthew Green's witty poem, *The Spleen*, 1737. Rarely heard after *c.* 1850; even *vent one's spleen*, to indulge one's bad temper, has been obsolescent since *c.* 1940.

2, Table-Book. A notebook; a memorandum-book. Obsolete by *c.* 1850.

3, 3, the Advice of Horace. Horace, *Ars Poetica*, 388, 'Nonumque prematur in annum' – Let it be held back, *or* kept quiet, until the ninth year. Thomas Creech's translation had appeared in 1684.

3a, paying the Postage. In Great Britain, where, as in other countries, the postal system grew out of the work performed by the king's messengers, regular rates were fixed as early as 1635. Rowland Hill's reorganization did not take effect until 1840.

4, Phrase. The term covers both idiomatic phrases and catch-phrases.

5, 5, Exercise of the Fan. This delicate aid to conversation and flirtation became a recognized weapon in the female armoury of London in the 17th century; the Restoration rendered it obligatory in Society; the 18th century regarded it as an established fact. In 1749 an anonymous writer published *The Fan: a heroi-comical poem in three cantos;* in 1785, William Cowper spoke of one who was 'grac'd with a sword, and worthier of a fan'.

6, *Bohemian* Woman; (a few lines later) the *Bohemian*. Gipsy; a Gipsy. The noun is recorded in Phillips's *Dictionary*, 1696; the adjective may here have made its first literary appearance.

6a, 6a, *Isaac* the Dancing-Master. This Frenchman, mentioned by Steele in *The Tatler* and by Southey in *The Doctor*, 'is best known by Soame Jenyns' couplet :
And Isaac's rigadoon shall live as long As Raphael's painting or as Virgil's song.' (Saintsbury).
A rigadoon was a lively, rather tricky dance for two persons.

7, Jargon-Terms. The learned words of the universities, a sense either coined or, at the least, established by 'Leviathan' Hobbes in 1651.

8, Cant-Words. Terms at once trivial, either slangy or very colloquial, ephemeral, and belonging to a class – here, apparently, that of London society.

9, the Honourable Colonel *James Graham*; 10, the late D— of R—; 11, E— of E—. Swift, I suspect, was pulling his readers' legs; but, even if he were not, I should agree with Saintsbury's comment, 'I do not know that attempts at identifying these shadowy personages would be very wise'. These three aristocratic figures, if they lived at all, apparently flourished in the 1680's and 1690's.

12, *Bite;* 13, *Bamboozle.* A *bite* is a deception, a trick, whereby one 'catches' someone in conversation. *Bamboozle,* to hoax, to 'catch', is of unknown origin : perhaps an imperfect blend of *baffle* and *banter* and *dazzle.* Compare (52).

14, the Lord and Lady *H*—. Compare notes 9–11.

15, hooted. Noisily derided. (Very slightly obsolescent.)

16, abbreviating. Only in the specific nuance defined by Swift himself – except that he included such an abbreviation as *plenipo*tentiary.

17, the Revolution. That of 1688.

18, Bishop *Burnet.* Gilbert Burnet (1643–1715), ecclesiastic and historian; vol. I of his *History of My Own Time* appeared in 1723; Swift thought its style as contemptible as its matter.

19, Bargains. To *sell* (someone) *a bargain* is to make a fool of him in conversation, to 'catch' him. (Originated by Shakespeare.) In Swift, especially a coarse reply to a question or a coarse comment on a remark.

20, Free-Thinking. The unrestrained – not necessarily *libertine* – exercise of reason in religious matters. In 1708, *The British Apollo* spoke of it as 'the modish phrase' *(OED).* Less pejorative in Swift's day than since *c.* 1840.

21, Blasphemy. This, on the other hand, was as strong a term in Swift's day as in ours.

22, Sprights. Spirits; especially ghosts. *Spright* is a variant of the obsolete *sprite,* itself a very English variant of *spirit.*

23, a famous Court-Chaplain. An ironic reference, either to Benjamin Hoadly (1676–1761), who, *c.* 1717, preached several free-thinking sermons, or to him and others like him, or merely to this kind of ecclesiastic.

24, the Fanatick Faction. The Puritans.

25, the Rumpers. Members of the 'Rump' Parliament – Puritans of 1653, 1659–60.

26, Enthusiasm. Extravagant and often misdirected religious emotion, especially as expressed in speech or writing. The great work on its manifestations in 17th–18th century England is Father Ronald Knox's *Enthusiasm,* 1950.

27, the *French* Huguenots. Protestants of the 16th–17th centuries. Swift is, of course, being ironic.

28, Double-entendres. Improper innuendoes; especially, double-meanings – the overt, unexceptionable; the covert, improper. The modern French word for a double-meaning is *double entente.*

29, Constraints. In the specific nuance : embarrassments.

30, Oaths. He does, in fact, introduce very few, and those mild.

31, Expletives to Matter. Words used to help fill out a sentence, or to fulfil a metre, without adding to the meaning.

32, an ancient Poet. 'I know him not, if he ever existed save as a maggot of Swift's brain' (Saintsbury). The couplet is very probably Swift's : he was no stranger to the device of 'putting over' something of one's own either under a fictitious name or, as here, with a deliberate, a generic, vagueness.

33, Annuals. As short-lived as annuals in the vegetable kingdom.

34, Sir *John Perrot*. He lived from 1527 (?) to 1592 and became Lord Deputy of Ireland. A brave soldier, he was so unfortunate, politically, that he died in the Tower of London.

35, by G—'s W—. By God's wounds (strictly, Christ's) – often slurred as *swounds* and especially *zounds*.

36, 36, one thousand, seventy and four. 1074. A characteristic Swiftian leg-pull. He knew that, as Dr Johnson was to say, 'Round numbers are always false', and that, as Carlyle once recorded, 'A witty statesman said, you might prove anything by figures'.

37, Romances. Novels preoccupied with adventure, sentiment and especially love – and love not, at this period, of the lower and lower-middle classes. Perhaps the earliest record of the word in this sense.

38, Grammar. The subject of English grammar was beginning to become popular among scholars and scholastic writers; the interest culminated, at least for the 18th century, in Bishop Lowth's work, *A Short Introduction to English Grammar*, 1762, a book that dominated the field for the next forty years or more. Compare :

39, *Lilly*. This is William Lilly, better Lily, who lived 1468 (?) – 1522; and the work is his too famous Latin Grammar, a 16th century remodelling and fusion of the *Rudimenta* of *c.* 1509 and the *Absolutissimus* of 1513. It tyrannized the teaching of Latin for two and a half centuries and vitiated that of English for nearly as long.

40, Projectors. Promoters – especially if shady – of public companies and private schemes.

41, Orthography. With this debasement of 'correct spelling' to 'any spelling', compare that of *calligraphy* from 'fine handwriting' to 'any handwriting'.

42, 42. Of all these colloquial shortenings, only 'e'n't' (ain't) does not now belong to correct familiar speech – that is, if we take 'coodn't and 'woodn't' to be merely scriptural variants of 'couldn't' and 'wouldn't'; 'e'n't' is dialectal – compare 'ben't' (bain't).

43, 43, Whereas 'jommetry and 'verdi' (variant 'vardi') are illiterate, 'larnin' is dialectal and 'lard' an affectation among the learned.

44, 45, 46, 47, 48, 49, 50, 51, 52. For (52), see (13). Of nos. 44–51, nos. 44 and 51 have been obsolete since *c.* 1800, and 50 since *c.* 1880 (hips) and 1800 (hippo); 48, little used since *c.* 1890; 46, 47, 49, are extant, the first of them rather 'dated' since *c.* 1940; and 45, as 'mob' (for 'mobile' for L. *mobile vulgus*), Standard English since *c.* 1820. Of similar more recent slang formations, 'swiz' for 'swindle' is a good example.

53, Chocolate-houses. Cafés where the staple beverage sold was chocolate; in England, they flourished *c.* 1655–1790, chocolate-drinking having been introduced at Oxford as early as 1650. What Oxford does today, London does tomorrow.

54, Black-pudding. Also called 'blood pudding' – a kind of sausage, made with blood and suet, usually with flour or meal added. German *Blutwurst*.

55, *Quadrille*. A four-handed game, played with forty (= 10 x 4) cards, introduced into England *c.* 1725, displacing ombre and, in turn, displaced by whist. (*OED*.)

55a, we are told. 'It may seem strange that Mr Wagstaff, who loves not books and scholars, should refer to a grave philosopher. But fine gentlemen in his youth had to know or seem to know their Hobbes', as Saintsbury remarks. The statement that 'a State of Nature . . . is a State of War' should read : 'The condition of man . . . is a condition of war of everyone against everyone'; it occurs in *Leviathan,* part I, chapter 4. Thomas Hobbes (1588–1679) did not possess an elegant style; he did possess a lucid and effective style.

56, 56, masquerading, Masquerade. Assemblies or balls at which the guests wear masks and are often disguised in other ways. They mostly disappeared in Queen Victoria's reign, during which Britons became much too serious for their own good.

57, Dialect. This is one of the earliest examples of *dialect* – a provincial mode of speech differing considerably from the educated standard applied to English.

58, 58, a Penny for your Thought. This is the predominant c. 16–mid c. 18 form of the proverbial saying 'A penny for your thoughts', recorded as early as 1762.

59, 59, well; but, to go on with my Story. How felicitously does Swift hit off the determined, I'll-finish what-I-have-to-say-or-die raconteur detested and dreaded by every good clubman !

60, St *James's*. Either generically the Court of St James's or specifically St James's Palace – the royal home until Queen Victoria invested Buckingham Palace with that honour.

61–67, Mr *Thomas Brown's* Works . . . the *Youngs*. All the writers named in this paragraph are treated ironically : whether, by excessive praise, to their disparagement or, by apparent depreciation, to their credit. The minnows become Tritons; the Tritons become 'that snarling Brood'.

Tom Brown (1633–1704) is best remembered for 'I do not love thee,

Doctor Fell'. Charles Gildon (1665–1724) was a miscellaneous writer, little more than a hack; Ned Ward (1667–1731), a much better miscellanist, a humorist – and valuable to students of English; John Dennis (1657–1734), a rather wooden and imperceptive critic. Whereas John Ozell (d. 1743) was a mediocre translator, Captain Stevens (John Stevens or Stephens, d. 1726) had served in the Irish campaign of 1689–91 and was a very able translator, an excellent Spanish and Portuguese scholar, and the author of a decidedly meritorious Spanish-English each-way dictionary and grammar, published in 1706. It is easy to see why Swift attacked the others with so savage an irony : but why pillory the inoffensive and self-effacing Stevens?

Pope, Gay, Arbuthnot, were Swift's friends; the poet Edward Young, an acquaintance.

68, the *Craftsman*. This periodical, which appeared first in December 1726 and lasted some ten years, consistently attacked Walpole and his cabinets. Swift and Arbuthnot contributed.

69, in sickly Pay-Day. An ironic pun on the French *encyclopédie*.

70, MUST, IS FOR THE KING. This aphorism ('Must is . . .') occurs very early in the first Conversation.

71, uncontroulable. Uncontrollable – in the obsolete sense 'irrefutable or incontrovertible'.

72, 72, Lord H——, . . . *Loyalty defined*. Is this Baron Hervey (John Hervey) – or a leg-pull?

73, Mr *Tibbalds,* or *Theobalds.* Lewis Theobald (1688–1744) may have been a literary hack, but he was certainly a Shakespearean editor of very great merit – one of the two or three best Shakespeare has ever had.

74, *Colly Cibber.* Colley Cibber (1671–1757) – Swift was rather (? deliberately) careless with names – wrote plays, ranging from bad to passable, and a very readable autobiography.

75, Embrio. A 16th–17th century rather than an 18th century spelling.

76, *Muscovy.* 'Russia', from 'the dukedom or province of Moscow', from 'the city of Moscow', from 'the river Moscow', from the Russian *Moskua.* The name Muscovy, deriving immediately from French *Muscovie* (earlier Moscovie), was current from *c*. 1570 until *c*. 1820, and then, except poetically, used only in certain combinations.

77, 77, *Charles XII,* late King of *Sweden.* He died in 1718, after a very successful reign of twenty years.

78, 79, one Isaac Newton, an Instrument-Maker . . . an obscure Mechanick. 'It is certainly probable that the reference to Sir Isaac Newton . . . was written after 1724, since it had been in the April of that year that he made his assay of Wood's copper money for Ireland, and reported that "it was of the same goodness and value with

the Copper . . . coined in the King's Mint for England" ' (Herbert
Davis) – a fact understandably failing to endear him to Swift.

80, 80, Answers, Repartees, Replies, and Rejoynders. Swift appears to
be satirizing his mouthpiece Wagstaff's verbosity rather than subtly
differentiating further than the generic 'answers' and collectively the
strictly distinguishable 'replies' (only slightly less generic than
'answers') and 'repartees' (sharp and witty) and 'rejoinders' (formal
and, originally, legal).

81, *not inglorious Memory*. Satirical of a stereotyped meiosis.

A Compleat Collection of
Genteel and Ingenious
Conversation

A COMPLEAT

COLLECTION

Of genteel and

Ingenious Conversation,

ACCORDING

To the most polite Mode and Method,
now used at Court, and in the
best Companies of *England*

In several dialogues

DUBLIN:
Printed by and for GEORGE FAULKNER
M,DCC,XXXVIII

The Men	*The Ladies*
Lord SPARKISH	
Lord SMART	Lady SMART
Sir JOHN LINGER	Miss NOTABLE
Mr. NEVEROUT	Lady ANSWERALL
Colonel ATWIT	

The ARGUMENT.

Lord Sparkish *and Colonel* Atwit *meet in the Morning upon the* Mall; *Mr.* Neverout *joins them; they all go to Breakfast at Lady* Smart's. *Their Conversation over their Tea: After which they part; but my Lord and the two Gentlemen are invited to Dinner. Sir* John Linger *invited likewise; and, comes a little too late. Their whole Conversation at Dinner: After which, the Ladies retire to their Tea. The Conversation of the Ladies without the Men; who are supposed to stay and drink a Bottle; but in some Time, go to the Ladies and drink Tea with them. The Conversation there. After which a Party at Quadrill until Three in the Morning; but no Conversation set down. They all take leave, and go Home.*

St. *James's Park*

[*Lord* Sparkish *meeting Colonel* Atwit.]

Colonel. **W**ELL met, my Lord.

Lord Sp. Thank ye Colonel; a Parson would have said, I hope we shall meet in Heaven. When did you see *Tom. Neverout?*

'a Parson . . . Heaven' : virtually a catch-phrase; not quite extinct.

Col. He's just coming towards us. Talk of the Devil.———

'Talk of the Devil' : in full, 'Talk of the Devil and he'll appear' or '. . . and he is sure to appear'; apparently since *c.* 1650; ultimately from Terence, 'De Varrone loquebamur; *lupus in fabula: venit enim ad me*'. (Apperson.)

[Neverout *comes up.*]

Col. How do you do *Tom?*

Nev. Never the better for you.

'Never the better for you' : now, None the better – or, No better – for your asking. (A catch-phrase.)

Col. I hope you're never the worse. But, where's your Manners? Don't you see my Lord *Sparkish?*

Nev. My Lord, I beg your Lordship's Pardon.

Lord Sp. Tom, How is it? what, you can't see the Wood for Trees? What Wind blew you hither?

'can't see the Wood for Trees' : this, the early form, has yielded to '. . . the trees'.

'What wind . . . hither?' : earliest in Chaucer.

Nev. Why, my Lord, it is an ill Wind that blows no Body Good; for it gives me the Honour of seeing your Lordship.

> 'ill wind . . . good' : first recorded by Heywood, 1546.

Col. Tom, you must go with us to Lady *Smart's* to Breakfast.
Nev. Must! why Colonel, *Must* is for the King.
> [*Colonel offering in jest to draw his Sword.*]

> '*Must* is for the King' : Only kings have the right to be so peremptory. Rare after the 18th century. (*ODEP.*)

Col. Have you spoke with all your Friends?

> 'spoke' : as past participle, common in the 14th–19th centuries; in in the 20th, archaic when not merely illiterate.

Nev. Colonel, as you are stout, be merciful.
Lord Sp. Come, agree, agree, the Law's costly.
> [*Colonel taking his Hand from the Hilt.*]
Nev. What, do you think I was born in a Wood to be scar'd by an Owl?

> 'What, do you think . . . Owl?' : apparently the earliest record – and apparently a contradiction – of the mostly rural proverb, now usually '(I live, He lives, etc.) too near the wood to be frightened by an owl (or, by owls)'. Apperson.

Col. Well *Tom,* you are never the worse Man for being afraid of me. Come along.
Nev. I'll wait on you. I hope Miss *Notable* will be there. I gad she's very handsome, and has Wit at Will.

> 'has Wit at Will' : can be witty whenever she pleases. Saintsbury refers to the constant late 16th–early 17th century 'jingles and plays on these two words . . . "Wit at will" survived most of its companions'. It survived until *c.* 1920.

Col. Why; every one as they like; as the good Woman said, when she kiss'd her Cow.

> 'every one . . . when she kiss'd her Cow' : a proverb dating from the early 16th century and usually 'Every man as he loveth, quoth the good man when he kissed his cow' (*ODEP*) : in short, everyone to his liking.

[*Lord* Smart's *House. They knock at the Door; Porter comes out.*]
Lord Sp. Pray are you the Porter?
Port. Yes, for Want of a better.
Lord Sp. Is your Lady at home?
Port. She was at home just now, but she is not gone out yet.

Nev. I warrant this Rogue's Tongue is well hung.

'this Rogue's Tongue . . .': he has a nimble tongue, or isn't tongue-tied.

[*Lady* Smart's *Anti-Chamber.*]
[*Lady* Smart, *and Lady* Answerall, *at the Tea-Table.*]

Lady Sm. My Lord, your Lordship's most humble Servant.

Lord Sp. Madam, you spoke too late, I was your Ladyship's before.

'Madam, you spoke . . .': a conventional or stock compliment.

Lady Sm. O! Colonel, are you here?

Col. As sure as you're there Madam.

Lady Sm. Oh, Mr. Neverout, what! such a Man alive!

Nev. Ay Madam, alive, and alive like to be, at your Ladyship's Service.

Lady Sm. Well, I'll get a Knife, and nick it down, that Mr. *Neverout* came to our House. And, pray what News Mr. *Neverout?*

'Well, I'll get a knife . . .': I must cut a notch, in order to record so notable an occasion.

Nev. News; why Madam, Queen *Elizabeth*'s dead.

'Queen *Elizabeth's* dead': the prototype of 'Queen Anne's dead', the latter occurring earliest in 1722 (Apperson), a mere eight years after Queen Anne died.

Lady Sm. Well, Mr. Neverout, I see you are no Changeling.

'. . . no Changeling': dependable. You can be counted on to say the expected thing, especially if it's the smart thing.

[*Miss* Notable *comes in.*]

Nev. Miss, your Slave; I hope your early Rising will do you no Harm: I find you are but just come out of the *Cloth-Market*.

'are but just come out of the *Cloth-Market*' (variant: 'have come . . .'): you have only just got out of bed, the *cloth market* being the bedclothes – hence, one's bed. Recorded earlier in the 1678 edition of John Ray's *English Proverbs*. Compare the 'go to bed' phrases on the last page but one of the dialogues.

Miss. I always rise at Eleven, whether it be Day or no.

Col. Miss, I hope you're up for all Day.

Miss. Yes, if I don't get a Fall before Night.

'get a Fall': fall down, slip. Physically.

Col. Miss, I heard you were out of Order. Pray how are you now?

'were out of Order': unwell, indisposed. Not seriousy ill.

Miss. Pretty well Colonel, I thank you.

> 'pretty well' : tolerably well. This adverbial use, dating from the 16th century, belongs to familiar – not to formal – Standard English. I always remember my father, on reading a University-prize essay of mine (I didn't win the prize) objecting to '*pretty good*'.

Col. Pretty, and Well, Miss, that's two very good Things.

Miss. I mean, I am better than I was.

Nev. Why, then 'tis well you were sick.

Miss. What, Mr. *Neverout,* you take me up, before I'm down.

> 'you take me up . . . down' : you 'catch' me before I fall or make a mistake.

Lord Sp. Come, let us leave off Children's Play, and go to Push-Pin.

> 'Push-Pin' : 'a child's play in which pins are pushed with an endeavour to cross them' (John Ash, *Dictionary*, 1775) : first in Shakespeare, *Love's Labour's Lost*, 1588. (*OED.*) Lord *Sparkish* was being sarcastic – unless perhaps he was making a bawdy pun.

Miss. [*to Lady* Smart] Pray Madam, give me some more Sugar to my Tea.

Col. Oh, Miss, you must needs be very good humoured, you love sweet Things so well.

> '. . . you love sweet Things so well' : sweet of tooth and temper. Neverout's 'the deeper the sweeter' is a proverbial phrase of the late 16th–20th centuries, but rare in the 20th and seldom recorded since the 18th. (Apperson.) I fear that this young blade was being very bawdy indeed.

Nev. Stir it up with the Spoon Miss, for the deeper the sweeter.

Lady Sm. I assure you, Miss, the Colonel has made you a great Compliment.

Miss. I am sorry for it; for I have heard 'em say, that Complimenting is lying.

> 'Complimenting is lying' : never quite becoming an accepted proverb.

Lady Sm. [*to Lord* Sparkish.] My Lord, methinks the Sight of you is good for sore Eyes : If we had known of your coming, we would have strown Rushes for you. How has your Lordship done this long Time?

> 'the Sight of you is good for sore Eyes' : now 'a sight for sore eyes', apparently recorded – at least, notably recorded first – by Hazlitt in 1838 (*ODEP*).

Col. Faith Madam, he's better in Health than good Condition.

> 'better in Health than good Condition': better than he looks – perhaps a shade too fat, yet healthy. Apparently a catch-phrase.

Lord Sp. Well; I see there's no worse Friend than one brings from Home with one; and I'm not the first Man that has carried a Rod to whip himself.

> 'there's no worse Friend . . .': Camden, 1605, 'Where shall a man have a worse friend than he brings from home?' (Apperson.) Common in the 17th–18th centuries; since, usually, 'A man's worst enemy is himself' – with anticipations throughout the earlier period.
> 'carried a Rod . . .': much commoner as 'to make a rod for one's own back'.

Nev. Here's poor Miss, has not a Word to throw at a Dog. Come, a Penny for your Thought.

> 'has not a Word . . .': does not know what to say. A proverb occurring first(?) in Shakespeare's *As You Like It*. For 'word' occasionally 'stone' (*ODEP*).
> 'a penny for your Thought': also in Swift's Introduction (my note 58). Miss Notable's smart reply is, one suspects, traditional: modern variant, 'They'd be dear at the price'.

Miss. It is not worth a Farthing; I was thinking of you.

[Colonel rising up.]

Lady Sm. Colonel, where are you going so soon? What, I hope you did not come to fetch Fire?

Col. Madam, I must needs go home for half an Hour.

Miss. Why, Colonel, they say the Devil's at home.

> 'the Devil's at home': cited as early as 1620, by dramatist Middleton, as a proverb.

Lady Answ. Well, but sit while you stay; 'tis as cheap sitting, as standing.

> ''tis as cheap sitting': why stand when you can sit?: 17th–20th centuries.

Col. No, Madam, while I'm *standing, I'm going.*

> 'while I'm *standing, I'm going*': able and ready to go; can very easily go. Apparently a smart catch-phrase of the time. Perhaps with implication 'am still alive'.

Miss. Nay, let him go, I promise we won't tear his Cloaths to hold him.

> 'Cloaths' for 'clothes' is a 16th–18th century spelling.

Lady Sm. I suppose, Colonel, we keep you from better Company; I mean only, as to my self.

Col. Madam, I'm all Obedience.

[*Colonel sits down.*]

Lady Sm. Lord, Miss, how can you drink your Tea so hot? Sure your Mouth is paved.

'your Mouth is paved' : hard and insensitive as if paved. A metaphor used still earlier.

Lady Sm. How do you like this Tea Colonel?

Col. Well enough, Madam, but methinks it is a little Morish.

'Morish' : 'moreish' – so good as to make one want more. A colloquialism apparently first recorded by Swift.

Lady Sm. Oh, Colonel, I understand you, *Betty* bring the Canister. I have but very little of this Tea left; but, I don't love to make two Wants of one, want when I have it, and want when I have it not. He, he, he, he. [*Laughs.*]

'two Wants' : earliest as 'I will not want when I have, and when I haven't too' (Ray, 1678); rare after *c.* 1800. The common restriction to Somerset is erroneous.

Lady Answ. [*To the Maid.*] Why, sure *Betty*, thou ar't bewitcht, this Cream is burnt too.

Betty. Why, Madam, the Bishop has set his Foot in it.

'the Bishop . . . in it' : 1528, Tyndale; obsolete since *c.* 1800, except in the English Midlands and North Country. Because the bishops used to have the authority to cause heretics to be burnt at the stake. (Apperson.)

Lady Sm. Go, run Girl, and warm some fresh Cream.

Betty. Indeed, Madam, there's none left, for the Cat has eaten it all.

Lady Sm. I doubt it was a Cat with two Legs.

'a Cat with two Legs' : the housewife's traditional reply to an errant servant; extant, especially as 'Yes; a cat with two legs'.

Miss. Colonel, don't you love Bread and Butter with your Tea?

Col. Yes, in a Morning Miss. For they say Butter is Gold in a Morning, and Silver at Noon, but it is Lead at Night.

'Butter is Gold . . . Night' : 16th–18th centuries. From its (alleged) stomachic effects.

Miss. The Weather is so hot, that my Butter melts on my Bread.

Lady Answ. Why, Butter I've heard 'em say, is mad twice a Year.

'Butter is mad twice a Year' : too soft in mid-summer and too cold in mid-winter : 17th–19th centuries. First recorded by Ben Jonson.

Lord Sp. [*To the Maid.*] Mrs. *Betty,* how does your Body politick?

> 'how does your Body politick?' : seemingly a rude catch-phrase, probably with a pun on the obsolete *body,* belly. Perhaps compare the low 20th century catch-phrase, 'How's your belly off for spots?'

Col. Fye, my Lord, you'll make Mrs. *Betty* blush.

Lady Sm. Blush! Ay, blush like a blue Dog.

> 'blush like a blue Dog' : a variant of the much commoner 16th–18th century proverbial saying, 'to blush like a black dog'.

Never. Pray, Mrs. *Betty,* are not you *Tom Johnson*'s Daughter?

Betty. So my Mother tells me, Sir.

> 'So my Mother tells me' : an extant catch-phrase that corresponds to the old proverb, 'Ask the mother if the child be like the father'.

Lord Sp. But, Mrs. *Betty,* I hear you are in Love.

Betty. My Lord, I thank GOD, I hate no Body, I am in Charity with all the World.

> 'in Charity with all the World' : well-disposed towards everybody.

Lady Sm. Why, Wench, I think thy Tongue runs upon Wheels this Morning. How came you by that Scratch on your Nose? Have you been fighting with the Cats?

> 'thy Tongue runs upon Wheels' : you're very talkative. The phrase dates from the 15th century. Compare the 16th–17th century proverb, 'Her tongue runs on pattens' and the 19th century, 'Your tongue runs nineteen to the dozen' – now the familiar 'to talk nineteen to the dozen' (Apperson; *ODEP*).

Col. [*to Miss*] Miss, when will you be married?

Miss. One of these odd-come-shortlies, Colonel.

> 'one of these odd-come-shortlies' : some day soon. Slang : an 18th–20th century catch-phrase; by *c.* 1920, obsolescent. It probably = 'one of these odd days shortly to come'.

Nev. Yes, they say the Match is half made; the Spark is willing, but Miss is not.

Miss. I suppose the Gentleman has got his own Consent for it.

Lady Answ. Pray my Lord, did you walk through the Park in this Rain?

Lord Sp. Yes, Madam, we were neither Sugar, nor Salt, we were not afraid the Rain would melt us, He, he, he. [*Laughs.*]

> 'neither Sugar, nor Salt, . . . afraid the Rain would melt us' : did not fear the rain – were neither delayed nor disconcerted by it. Extant, although by 1945 slightly archaic.

Col. It rained, and the Sun shone at the same Time.

Never. Why, then the Devil was beating his Wife behind the Door with a Shoulder of Mutton. [*Here a loud Laugh.*]

> 'the Devil . . . a Shoulder of Mutton' : the second part of a 17th–20th (latterly rural only) proverb, 'When it rains and the sun shines at the same time'. Richard Inwards, *Weather Lore,* 1893, 'He is laughing and she is crying'. (Apperson.)

Col. A blind Man would be glad to see that.

> 'A blind man . . .' : That would be a fine sight. Probably derives from the much older 'Would I could see it, quoth blind Hugh', occurring in this Conversation.

Lady Sm. Mr. *Neverout,* methinks you stand in your own Light.

> 'stand in your own Light' : a 16th–20th century phrase that, from being proverbial, has become a common metaphor.

Never. Ah, Madam, I have done so all my Life.

Lord Sp. I am sure he sits in mine : Prithee *Tom,* sit a little further, I believe your Father was no Glazier.

> 'your Father was no Glazier' has the modern variant '. . . a bad glazier'.

Lady Sm. Miss, dear Girl, fill me a Dish of Tea; for I'm very lazy.

> 'Dish of Tea' : a cup of tea; compare *tea-dish,* an 18th century name for a tea-cup.

[*Miss fills a Dish of Tea, sweetens it, and then tastes it.*]

Lady Sm. What, Miss, will you be my Taster?

Miss. No, Madam, but they say, she's an ill Cook that can't lick her her own Fingers.

> 'ill Cook . . . Fingers' : a 16th–20th century proverb (Shakespeare and Scott use it) – rare in the 20th.

Never. Pray, Miss, fill me another.

Miss. Will you have it now, or stay till you get it?

> 'Will you have . . . get it?' : a 17th–20th century catch-phrase, the 19th–20th form being '. . . wait . . .'.

Lady Answ. But, Colonel, they say, you went to Court last Night very drunk : Nay, I am told for certain, you had been among the *Philistians.* No Wonder the Cat winked, when both her Eyes were out.

> 'the *Philistians*' : a 14th–early 18th century variant of *Philistines* in the slangy, humorous 17th–18th century sense 'the drunks and

the debauchees'. From the warlike ancient Philistines, traditional foes of the Israelites.

'the Cat winked, when both her Eyes were out' : 17th–18th centuries : the 16th century form being '. . . when her eye was out'. There is an allusion to the idea *blind* drunk'.

Col. Indeed, Madam, that's a Lye.

Lady Answ. Well, 'tis better I should lye, than you should lose your Manners. Besides, I don't lye, I sit.

Lady *Answerall* delivers herself both of a reproof and of a punning retort ('I don't lye, I sit') that has never, I think, quite become a catch-phrase.

Never. O faith, Colonel, you must own you had a Drop in your Eye; for when I left you, you were half Seas over.

'had a Drop in your Eye' and 'were half Seas over' : to be a little drunk. Both phrases – the former, now obsolescent – date from the late 17th century; the latter, originally nautical slang.

Lord Sp. Well, I fear Lady *Answerall,* can't live long, she has so much Wit.

Never. No, she can't live, that's certain; but she may linger thirty or forty Years.

Miss. Live long ! Ay, longer than a Cat, or a Dog, or a better Thing.

Lady Answ. Oh, Miss, you must give your *Vardi* too.

'you must give your *Vardi* too' : must have your say. (*Vardi* or *verdi* = verdict.)

Lord Sp. Miss, shall I fill you another Dish of Tea?

Miss. Indeed, my Lord, I have drank enough.

'I have drank enough' : *drank,* as past participle, belongs to the 17th–19th centuries; in the 20th, increasingly regarded as illiterate.

Lord Sp. Come, it will do you more Good than a Month's fasting. Here, take it.

Miss. No, I thank your Lordship, enough's as good as a Feast.

'enough's . . . a Feast' : dating from the 15th century (and earlier), this proverb belongs to the world's common stock. Compare the 16th–20th century variant, 'Enough is enough' and the genteel phrase, 'an elegant sufficiency'.

Lord Sp. Well, but if you always say no, you'll never be married.

Lady Answ. Do, my Lord, give her a Dish, for they say Maids will say no, and take it.

'Maids will say No . . .' : an old saying, with numerous slight variants. Compare Shakespeare's 'Play the maid's part, still answer nay, and take it' (*Richard the Third*, III, vii).

Lord Sp. Well, and I dare say, Miss is a Maid in Thought, Word and Deed.

Never. I would not take my Oath of that.

Miss. Pray, Sir, speak for your self.

Lady Sm. Fye, Miss: Maids, they say, should be seen, and not heard.

> 'Maids should be seen . . .': *c*. 1400, already 'an old Englysch sawe'. In the 19th century, often 'Little girls . . .'; in the 20th, obsolete.

Lady Answ. Good Miss, stir the Fire, that the Tea-Kettle may boyl. You have done it very well, now it burns purely. Well, Miss, you'll have a chearful Husband.

Miss. Indeed, your Ladyship could have stirred it much better.

Lady Answ. I know that very well Hussy, but I won't keep a Dog, and bark my self.

> 'I won't keep a Dog . . .': dating from the 16th century and, especially as 'to keep a dog and bark oneself', still current. To employ someone and yet do his work.

Never. What; you are stuck Miss?

> 'you are stuck, Miss?': at a loss for an answer.

Miss. Not at all, for her Ladyship meant you.

Nev. O, faith Miss, you are in Lob's Pound, get out as you can.

> 'in Lob's Pound': in an inextricable difficulty. Lob's pound also = a prison. After *c*. 1820, rare except in dialect. Who Lob was, we don't know – probably because no such person ever existed.

Miss. I won't quarrel with my Bread and Butter, for all that; I know when I'm well.

> 'quarrel with my Bread and Butter': usually, with one's livelihood; here, perhaps, object to the refreshment I receive.

Lady Answ. Well, but Miss.

> 'Well, but Miss': Well, yes; but with reservations.

Nev. Ah, dear Madam, let the Matter fall; take Pity upon poor Miss; don't throw Water on a drounded Rat.

> 'don't throw Water . . .': don't kick anyone when he's down. Also 'Pour not' – or, 'Don't pour' – 'water on a drowned mouse'. (*ODEP*) – The form *drownded*, dialectal here, has long been illiterate when not dialectal.

Miss. Indeed Mr. *Neverout*, you should be cut for the Simples this

Morning. Say a Word more, and you had as good eat your Nails.

> 'cut for the Simples' : cured of your folly. A 17–19th century pun on *simple* (-minded) and *simples,* curative herbs.
> 'eat your Nails' : bite your nails. Rare after *c.* 1800.

Lord Sp. Pray Miss, will you please to favour us with a Song?
Miss. Indeed my Lord I can't; I have got a great Cold.
Col. Oh Miss, they say all good Singers have Colds.

> 'all good Singers have Colds' : an excuse for not singing unpaid or to an unappreciative audience.

Lord Sp. Pray Madam, does not Miss sing very well?
Lady Answ. She sings, as one may say; my Lord.

> 'She sings, as one may say' : Well, you *could* say so.

Miss. I hear Mr. *Neverout* has a very good Voice.
Col. Yes, *Tom* sings well; but his Luck's naught.
Nev. Faith, Colonel, there you hit yourself a devilish Box of the Ear.
Col. Miss, will you take a Pinch of Snuff?
Miss. No, Colonel, you must know, I never take Snuff but when I'm angry.

> 'never take Snuff but when I'm angry' : an allusive pun on the 16th–18th century phrase *take in snuff,* or *take snuff,* to take offence.

Lady Answ. Yes, yes, she can take Snuff, but she has never a Box to put it in.

> 'take Snuff, but . . . never a Box to put it in' : will accept an offer of snuff, but never carries it herself.

Miss. Pray Colonel let me see that Box?
Col. Madam, there's never a C. upon it.

> '. . . let me see that Box? – Madam, there's never a C. upon it' : a pun, 'see . . . C' – as in the Comic Phonetic Alphabet, 'C for yourself'; probably on 'C[olonel]'; and perhaps as in Sterne's 'C—'.

Miss. May be there is Colonel.
Col. Ay, but *May-bees* don't fly now Miss.

> 'May be there is Colonel. – Ay, but *May-bees* don't fly now' : a pun on *may be,* perhaps, and 'a *May* bee'. Usually 'May-bees don't fly this month'; although not often heard in the 20th century, it is far from being obsolete. Compare the long-obsolete 'Every *may be* hath a *may not be*'. (Apperson.)

Nev. Colonel, why so hard upon poor Miss? Don't set your Wit against a Child: Miss give me a Blow, and I'll beat him.

'Don't set your Wit . . .': Don't take an unfair advantage.
'Miss, give me a Blow, and I'll beat him': either 'Give me a little encouragement . . .' or 'Punch me, and, in anger, I'll beat him'.

Miss. So she pray'd me to tell you.
Lord Sp. Pray, my Lady *Smart,* what Kin are you to Lord *Pozz?*
Lady Sm. Why, his Grandmother and mine had four Elbows.

'His Grandmother and mine had four Elbows': We are both human beings – there's no closer relationship than that. Probably a catch-phrase that never became very widely used.

Lady Answ. Well; methinks here's a silent Meeting. Come Miss, hold up your Head Girl, there's Money bid for you. [*Miss starts.*]

'here's a silent Meeting': perhaps an allusion to a Friends' *meeting* (an assembly for worship).
'there's money bid for you': you are being observed; you are in request. Marryat, 1836, has 'As the saying is, there's . . .'. (Apperson.)

Miss. Lord, Madam, you frighten me out of my seven Senses!

'frighten me out of my seven Senses': more emphatic than the customary five; *frighten out of one's senses* (or *wits*) is the commonest form. 'Scared out of her seven senses': Motteux, 1694. (*OED.*)

Lord Sp. Well, I must be going.
Lady Answ. I have seen hastier People than you stay all Night.

'hastier People than you stay all Night': those who, apparently eager to depart, wish to be urged to stay.

Col. [*to Lady Smart.*] *Tom Neverout* and I, are to leap Tomorrow for a Guinea.
Miss. I believe Colonel, Mr. *Neverout* can leap at a Crust better than you.
Nev. Miss, your Tongue runs before your Wit: Nothing can tame you but a Husband.

'your Tongue runs before your Wit': you speak without thinking. Foreshadowed in the 14th century and current in the 16th–18th. (Apperson.)

Miss. Peace, I think I hear the Church Clock.
Nev. Why, you know as the Fool thinks, the Bell chinks.

'as the Fool thinks, the Bell chinks': a 17th–19th century proverb, foreshadowed in the 14th. 'He that hears bells, will make them sound what he list' (pleases) : 'Melancholy' Burton, 1621 (*ODEP*).

Lady Sm. Mr. *Neverout,* your Handkerchief's fallen.

Miss. Let him set his Foot upon it, that it mayn't fly in his Face.

Nev. Well Miss.

Miss. Ay, ay, many a One says *Well,* that thinks *Ill.*

> 'many a One says *Well* . . .' : clearly a proverb, but, so far as we know, recorded only here.

Nev. Well Miss, I'll think of this.

Miss. That's Rhyme, if you take it in Time.

Nev. What ! I see you are a Poet.

Miss. Yes, if I had but Wit to shew it.

> 'That's Rhyme, if you take it in Time.
> 'What ! I see you are a Poet.
> 'Yes, if I had but Wit to shew it.' (Or, in the 19th–20th century, 'but don't know it'.)
> These three speeches go to form a crambo, or set of rhymes made in the game of crambo, 'in which one player gives a word or line of verse to which each of the others has to find a rime' (*OED.*) – earlier *crambe,* itself from Latin *crambe repetita*; popular throughout the 17th–early 18th century.

Nev. Miss, will you be so kind to fill me a Dish of Tea ?

Miss. Pray let your Betters be served before you; I am just going to fill one for my self : And, you know the Parson always christens his own Child first.

> 'Parson christens his own Child first' : a mid-17th–20th century proverb (with variant, in the 17th : 'priest') that represents an apologetic 'Charity begins at home'.

Nev. But, I saw you fill one just now for the Colonel : Well, I find Kissing goes by Favour.

> 'Kissing goes by Favour' : 17th–20th centuries. Broad application : 'We favour most those we like best'.

Col. Ods so, I have cut my Thumb with this cursed Knife.

Lady Answ. Ay, that was your Mother's Fault; because she only warned you not to cut your Fingers.

Lady Sm. No, no; 'tis only Fools cut their Fingers, but wise Folks cut their Thumbs.

> 'Fools cut their Fingers, but wise Folks cut their Thumbs' : this late 17th–20th century proverb (rare in the 20th) has variant 'wise men'. Sense : 'the follies of the wise are prodigious' (Vincent

Stuckey Lean, *Collectanea*, 4 vols., 1902–4, cited by *ODEP*); they do things – even stupid things – in a big way.

Miss. I'm sorry for it, but I can't cry. But pray, Mr. *Neverout*, what Lady was that you were talking with in the Side-box last *Tuesday?*

'sorry . . . but I can't cry' : earliest (1584), 'I am sorry for thee, but I cannot weep'; extant, but now usually modified to suit the speaker's fancy.

'Side-box' : an enclosed set of seats – a box – at the side of a theatre.

Nev. Miss; can you keep a Secret?
Miss. Yes, I can.
Nev. Well Miss, and so can I.

'can you keep a Secret? . . . so can I' : a 'catch'.

Col. Don't you think Miss is grown?
Lady Answ. Ay, ay, ill Weeds grow a-pace.

'ill Weeds grow a-pace' : dating from the 15th century and still common.

Miss. No, Madam, with Submission, 'tis Weeds of Grace that grow a-pace.

[*A Puff of Smoak comes down the Chimney.*]
Lady Answ. Lord Madam! does your Ladyship's Chimney smoak?
Col. No Madam, but they say Smoak always pursues the Fair, and your Ladyship sat nearest.

'Smoak always pursues the Fair' : a 17th–20th century proverb, but in the 19th–20th mostly rural.

Lady Sm. Madam, do you love Bohea Tea?

'Bohea Tea' (pronounced *bo-hee*) : originally superior black tea : the Chinese *Wu-i cha*, the *cha* or tea from the *Wu-i* or hills north of Fukhien, one of the best tea-growing regions of China. In English, recorded first (*OED*) in 1704; has long been slang, in the form *char*.

Lady Answ. Why really Madam, I must confess, I do love it; but it does not love me.

'I do love it . . .' : now usually in the form 'I like it, but it doesn't like me'.

Miss. [*to Lady* Smart.] Indeed Madam, your Ladyship is very sparing of your Tea; I protest, the last Dish I took, was no more than Water bewitcht.

'Water bewitcht' : very weak tea; originally of beer or wine much-diluted.

Col. Pray Miss, if I may be so bold, what Lover gave you that fine Etuy?

'Etuy': an 18th (as *ettuy* is a 17th) century form of the 17th–20th century *etwee* or *etui* (Fr. *étui*): a (very) small, usually ornamented, case for such things as needles.

Miss. Don't you know? then keep Council.

'keep Council': keep counsel – say nothing.

Lady Answ. I'll tell you Colonel who gave it her; it was the best Lover she will ever have while she lives; even her own dear Papa.

'the best Lover . . . Papa': now, 'A girl's best friend is her father'.

Nev. Methinks Miss, I don't much like the Colour of that Ribband.

'Ribband': a 16th–19th century form of *ribbon*; like *riband*, archaic by *c.* 1850.

Miss. Why then, Mr. *Neverout,* if you don't like it, dy'e see, you may look off of it.

'if you don't like it . . . you may look off of it': now, '. . . you lump it' (put up with it); *off of* = away from (You may look the other way).

Lord Sp. I don't doubt Madam, but your Ladyship has heard that Sir *John Bearish,* has got an Employment at Court.

Lady Sm. Yes, yes, and I warrant he thinks himself no small Fool now.

'thinks himself no small Fool': thinks well of himself. Compare the 19th–20th century 'thinks no small beer of himself'.

Nev. Yet, Madam, I have heard some People take him for a wise Man.

Lady Sm. Ay, some are Wise, and some are otherwise.

'. . . Wise, and . . . otherwise': half-way between a pun and a proverb, this saying is still heard occasionally. Apperson records it for 1659.

Lady Answ. Do you know him Mr. *Neverout?*

Nev. Know him; ay Madam as well as a Beggar knows his Dish.

'as well as . . . Dish': very well indeed. Arising early in 16th, obsolete by mid-19th century. Here, *dish* is elliptical for *alms-dish*.

Col. Well, I can only say he has better Luck than honester Folks: But, pray how came he to get this Employment?

Lord Sp. Why, by Chance, as the Man killed the Devil.

'by Chance, as . . . the Devil': a proverb that has not survived.

Nev. Why Miss, you are in a brown Study. What's the Matter; methinks you look like Mum chance, that was hang'd for saying nothing.

> 'in a brown Study': gloomily, or concentratedly, thoughtful. Probably suggested by the now obsolete *brown* = gloomy.
> 'Mum chance . . . saying nothing': *mumchance* (obsolete), dogged silence, hence one who keeps doggedly silent. The proverb belongs to the 16th–18th centuries.

Miss. I'd have you to know I scorn your Words.

Nev. Well, ay but scornful Dogs, they say, will eat dirty Puddings.

> 'scornful Dogs . . . dirty puddings': late 17th–mid-19th century.

Miss. Well, my Comfort is, your Tongue's no slander. What, you would not have one be always upon the high Grin?

> 'your Tongue's no slander': you don't slander yourself.
> 'upon the high Grin': grinning broadly.

Nev. Cry Mapsticks, Madam, no Offence I hope.

> 'Cry Mapsticks': 'I do not understand "Mapsticks", remarks Saintsbury. *Mapstick* = *mopstick,* a mop's long handle. The phrase, as *The OED* says, is apparently 'a vulgar jocose version of "I cry you mercy"'. But perhaps Neverout, being even more heartless than usual, is saying, 'Cry to your heart's content, Madam – no offence, I hope': compare the Warwickshire *look like death on a mopstick,* to look utterly miserable.

> [*Lady* Smart *breaks a Tea-cup.*]

Lady Answ. Lord, Madam, how came you to break your Cup?

Lady Sm. I can't help it, if I would cry my Eyes out.

> 'I can't help it . . .': weeping won't help.

Miss. Why sell it, Madam, and buy a new one with some of the Money.

Col. Why, if Things do not break or wear out, how should Tradesmen live?

Miss. Well, I'm very sick, if any Body cared for it. [*She spits.*] I believe I shall dye, for I can't spit from me.

> 'Well, I'm very sick . . . spit from me': As if anyone cares! . . . I can't spit any distance.

Nev. Come then, Miss, e'en make a Die of it; and then we shall have a burying of our own.

> 'e'en make a Die of it': go ahead and die.

Miss. The Devil take you, *Neverout,* besides all small Curses.

Lady Answ. Marry come up: What, plain *Neverout,* methinks you might have an M under your Girdle, Miss.

> 'Marry come up': Oh, come now! (Amused surprise.) Already archaic at the time.
> 'have an M under your Girdle': You might have addressed him as 'Mr' — the *M* being short for '*M*aster' or '*M*istress' or '*M*iss'. Also *carry an M* . . . Compare the 20th century '*Mister* to you'.

Lady Sm. Well, well; naught's ne'er in Danger, I warrant, Miss will spit in her Hand and hold fast. Colonel, do you like this Bisket?

> 'spit . . . and hold fast'. To spit on one's hands in order to get a better grip.
> 'Bisket': a common 16th–18th century spelling of *biscuit.*

Col. I'm like all Fools, I love every Thing that's good.

> 'like all Fools, I love . . .': a catch-phrase, extant in one form or another. *ODEP* gives it as a proverb in the form, 'I am a fool: I love anything (everything) that is good'.

Lady Sm. Well and isn't it pure good?

Col. 'Tis better than a worse.

> 'better than a worse': another catch-phrase, I think. 'It might be worse.'

[*Footman brings the Colonel a Letter.*]

Lady Answ. I suppose, Colonel, that's a Billet-doux from your Mistress.

> 'Billet-doux': a loving note, a love-letter. Since *c.* 1880, mostly humorous.

Col. I'gad I don't know whence it comes, but whoever writ it, writes a Hand like a Foot.

> 'writes a Hand like a Foot': writes largely and clumsily, a horrible scrawl. By *c.* 1900, obsolescent; yet, even by the 1960s, not obsolete.

Miss. Well you may make a Secret of it, but we can spell and put together.

Nev. Miss, what spells B double uzzard?

> 'uzzard': a variant – long illiterate, when not dialectal – of *izzard,* itself now dialectal for the letter z.

Miss. Buzzard in your Teeth, Mr. *Neverout.*

Lady Sm. Mr. *Neverout,* now you are up, will you do me the Favour to do me the Kindness to take off the Tea-Kettle.

Lord Sp. I wonder what makes these Bells ring?

Lady Answ. Why my Lord, I suppose because they pull the Ropes. [*Here all laugh.*]

[Neverout *plays with a Tea-cup*.]

Miss. Now a Child would have cryed half an Hour before he could have found out such a pretty Play-Thing.

Lady Sm. Well said, Miss: I vow Mr. *Neverout,* the Girl is too hard for you.

'too hard for you' : too sharp and witty; too smart.

Nev. Ay, Miss will say any Thing but her Prayers, and those she whistles.

'say anything but her Prayers . . . whistles' : partly a proverb, partly a catch-phrase, of the late 17th–mid-19th century. Never says them.

Miss. Pray, Colonel, make me a Present of that pretty Knife.

'a Present of that pretty Knife . . . it will cut Love' : an allusion to the very old superstition that one should never give anything sharp to one's beloved – at least, before marriage.

Nev. Ay, Miss, catch him at that, and hang him.

Col. Not for the World, dear Miss, it will cut Love.

Lord Sp. Colonel, you shall be married first, I was just going to say that.

'You shall be married first' : another piece of folk-lore.

Lady Sm. Well, but for all that, I can tell you who is a great Admirer of Miss: Pray, Miss, how do you like Mr. *Spruce,* I swear I have seen him often cast a Sheep's Eye out of a Calve's Head at you, deny it if you can.

'cast a Sheep's Eye out of a Calve's Head at you' : earliest and usually *cast a sheep's eye* : 16th–20th centuries. A sheep has a large, soft, liquid eye. Here, *calve's* for *calf's* merely indicates a slovenly pronunciation.

Miss. O Madam, all the World knows, that Mr. *Spruce* is a general Lover.

'a general Lover' : very fond of the ladies.

Col. Come, Miss, it is too true to make a Jest on. [*Miss blushes.*]

Lady Answ. Well, however blushing is some Sign of Grace.

'blushing is some Sign of Grace' : a 16th–18th century proverb, with several variants, especially 'a sign of virtue'. Francis Bacon, in 1605, quotes a Latin original : *Rubor est virtutis color (ODEP)*.

Nev. Miss says nothing, but I warrant she pays it off with thinking.

'Miss says nothing, but . . .' : a late 17th–19th century variant of a very old phrase, *to say nothing but think the more* (or . . . *think much*) or *think much and* (or *but*) *say little* (or *nothing*) : compare Lydgate's 'thynk mekyl [=much] and sey nought'. (Apperson.)

Miss. Well, Ladies and Gentlemen, I find you are pleased to divert your selves; but as I hope to be saved there is nothing in it.

'as I hope to be saved' (from Hell) : one of the oldest pious wishes.

Lady Sm. Ah, Miss, Love will creep where it can't go : They say, touch a gall'd Horse, and he'll wince.

'Love will creep . . .' : with variant '. . . may not go', it dates from the 14th century; but, except in dialect, rare since *c.* 1850. 'Love will find a way.'
'a gall'd Horse' : 14th–20th century; immortalized in Shakespeare's allusive 'Let the galled jade wince, our withers are unwrung' ('So-and-so you, Jack, *I*'m all right').

Miss. I'd hold a hundred Pound Mr. *Neverout* was the Inventor of that Story; and, Colonel, I doubt you had a Finger in the Pye.

'a Finger in the Pye' : a 16th (? earlier)–20th century phrase.

Lady Answ. But, Colonel, you forgot to salute Miss when you came in; she said, you had not seen her a long Time.

'to salute Miss' : to greet her with a kiss : an 18th–20th century usage, increasingly archaic since *c.* 1870.

Miss. Fye, Madam, I vow, Colonel, I said no such Thing; I wonder at your Ladyship.

Col. Miss, I beg your Pardon.

[*Goes to salute her, she struggles a little.*]

Miss. Well, I had rather give a Knave a Kiss for once, than be troubled with him : But, upon my Word, you are more bold than welcome.

'give a Knave a Kiss' : a variant of the 17th–18th century proverb, 'It is better to kiss a knave (for once) than to be troubled with him'.
'more bold than welcome' : mid-16th–18th centuries. *Bold*, over-familiar.

Lady Sm. Fye, fye, Miss, for Shame of the World, and Speech of good People.

[*Neverout to Miss, who is cooking her Tea and Bread and Butter.*]

'*cooking her Tea and Bread and Butter*' : '(as I suppose), putting the bread-and-butter in the tea. I believe this atrocious practice is not absolutely obsolete yet' (Saintsbury, 1892) – no, not yet. A sense apparently ignored by the dictionaries.

Nev. Come, come, Miss, make much of naught, good Folks are scarce.

'good Folks are scarce': Make do with what you have: good men are scarce. The latter half is a 17th–20th century proverb, addressed mostly to women. The women usually retort, 'But not so scarce as all *that*!'

Miss. What, and you must come in with your two Eggs a Penny, and three of them rotten.

'come in with your two Eggs a Penny, and . . .': seldom heard nowadays, this witty proverb has the variant 'five eggs, and four of them rotten'. Compare the 20th century addition to 'Two fools are born every minute' (or 'There are two . . .'): 'and you are three of them'.

Col. [*To Lord* Sparkish.] But, my Lord, I forgot to ask you, how you like my new Cloaths?

Lord Sp. Why, very well, Colonel, only to deal plainly with you, methinks the worst Piece is in the Middle.

'very well . . . the worst Piece is in the Middle': the worst part is the man inside them. Apperson cites a Gloucestershire variant dated 1639: 'All is well save that the worst piece is in the midst'.

[*Here a loud Laugh often repeated.*]

Col. My Lord, you are too severe on your Friends.

Miss. Mr. *Neverout,* I'm hot, are you a Scot?

Nev. Miss, I'm cold, are you a Scold? Take you that.

'I'm hot, are you a Scot? – Miss, I'm cold, are you a Scold?': a variant of the crambo, which, by the way, is the original of the late 1950s – early 1960s type of wit exemplified by 'What o'clock, cock?' and 'How's your thumb, chum?'
'Take you that': Put that in your pipe and smoke it.

Lady Sm. I confess that was home: I find, Mr. *Neverout,* you won't give your Head for the washing, as they say.

'won't give your Head for the washing': as Saintsbury has noted, from the French *laver la tête à quelqu'un,* to scold him: a Gallicism that failed to 'catch on'.

Miss. O, he's a sore Man where the Skin's off: I see Mr. *Neverout* has a Mind to sharpen the Edge of his Wit on the Whetstone of my Ignorance.

'a sore Man when the Skin's off': Let the galled jade wince!
'sharpen the Edge . . . Ignorance': a quotation? Too laboured to be a proverb, it was just possibly a catch-phrase.

Lord Sp. Faith *Tom,* you are struck; I never heard a better Thing.

Nev. Pray, Miss, give me Leave to scratch you for that fine Speech.

'give me Leave to Scratch you' : as a woman scratches.

Miss. Pox on your Picture, it cost me a Groat the drawing.

'Pox on your Picture . . .' : It cost me nothing to 'tell you where to get off'. The oath was, even in those days, a trifle coarse for a lady.

Nev. [To *Lady* Smart.] 'Sbuds, Madam, I have burnt my Hand with your plaguy Tea-Kettle.

' 'Sbuds' : 'sbodikins : God's bodikins. 'plaguy' : pestilent or accursed, in weakened sense.

Lady Sm. Why then, Mr. *Neverout,* you must say, God save the King.

'you must say, God save the King' : folk-lore.

Nev. Did you ever see the like?

Miss. Never but once at a Wedding.

'Never but once at a Wedding' : either a proverbial phrase or a catch-phrase of *c.* 1650–1750.

Col. Miss, pray how old are you?

Miss. Why, I am as old as my Tongue, and a little older than my Teeth.

'as old as my Tongue . . . Teeth' : apparently first recorded by Swift; extant.

Lord Sp. [*To Lady* Answerall.] Pray, Madam, is Miss *Buxom* marry'd? I hear it is all over the Town.

Lady Answ. My Lord, she's either marry'd, or worse.

'either marry'd, or worse' : either wife or mistress.

Col. If she ben't marry'd, at least she's lustily promised. But is it certain that Sir *John Blunderbuz* is dead at last?

'lustily' : either 'heartily' or perhaps 'cheerfully'.

Lord Sp. Yes, or else he's sadly wrong'd; for they have bury'd him.

'sadly wrong'd' : gravely wronged.

Miss. Why, if he be dead, he'll eat no more Bread.

'if he be dead . . . Bread' : a jingle, not (I believe) a proverb.

Col. But is he really dead?

Lady Answ. Yes, Colonel, as sure as you're alive.

'as sure as you're alive' : wittier than most of Lady Answerall's remarks. Variant: '. . . as I'm alive' – which the superstitious avoid.

Col. They say he was an honest Man.
Lady Answ. Yes, with good looking to.

'with good looking to' : provided that he was closely watched.

[*Miss feels a Pimple on her Face.*]

Miss. Lord, I think my Goodness is coming out : Madam, will your Ladyship please to lend me a Patch?

'my Goodness is coming out' : pimply because virtuous.

Nev. Miss, if you are a Maid, put your Hand upon your Spot.

'if you are a Maid . . .' : one suspects a rakish double-meaning.

Miss. There, [*covering her whole Face with both her Hands.*]
Lady Sm. Well, thou art a mad Girl. [*Gives her a Tap.*]
Miss. Lord, Madam, is that a Blow to give a Child?
[*Lady* Smart *lets fall her Handkerchief, and the Colonel stoops for it.*]
Lady Sm. Colonel, you shall have a better Office.

'have a better Office' : be better employed.

Col. Oh, Madam, I can't have a better than to serve your Ladyship.
Col. [*To Lady* Sparkish] Madam, has your Ladyship read the new Play written by a Lord, it is called, *Love in a hollow Tree?*

'Play written by a Lord' : Lord Grimston (satirized by Pope as 'booby Lord') is said to have written it when he was aged fourteen. Published in 1705, William Luckyn, Viscount Grimston's *The Lawyer's Fortune. Love in a Hollow Tree* was a five-act prose comedy.

Lady Sp. No, Colonel.
Col. Why then, your Ladyship has a new Pleasure to come.

'a new Pleasure to come' : a new sort of pleasure.

[*Miss sighs.*]

Nev. Pray, Miss, why do you sigh?
Miss. To make a Fool ask, and you are the first.

'To make a Fool ask . . . first' : a catch-phrase, extant (although not very common) in one form or another.

Nev. Why, Miss, I find there is nothing but a Word and a Blow with you.

'a Word and a Blow' : 16th–20th centuries. Benjamin Franklin, in 1768, wrote that 'It is said of choleric people, that with them there is but a word and a blow' : it needs but one word to cause a blow.

Lady Answ. Why, you must know, Miss is in Love.

Miss. I wish my Head may never ake till that Day.

'Head may never ake till that Day' : lucky if I have no headache until then. A catch-phrase.

Lord Sp. Come, Miss, never sigh but send for him.

'never sigh but send for him' : also simply 'Never sigh, but send' (17th–19th centuries) – 'Spoken when a young maid sighs, alleging that it is for a sweetheart' (J. Kelly, *A Complete Collection of Scotish Proverbs,* 1721) (*ODEP*).

[*Lady* Smart, *and Lady* Answerall, *speaking together.*]
If he be hang'd he'll come hopping, and if he be drown'd, he'll come dropping.

'If he be hang'd . . . dropping' : another jingle.

Miss. Well, I'll swear you'd make one dye with laughing.

[*Miss plays with a Tea-cup, and Neverout plays with another.*]

Nev. Well, I see one Fool makes many.

'one Fool makes many' : already in 1617 described as an old proverb; rare after *c.* 1890. Miss Neverout's retort goes to make crambo.

Miss. And you're the greatest Fool of any.

Nev. Pray, Miss, will you be so kind to tye this String for me, with your fair Hands? It will go all in your Day's work.

Miss. Marry come up indeed; tye it your self, you have as many Hands as I, your Man's Man will have a fine Office truly. Come, pray stand out of my spitting Place.

'tye it yourself, you have as many Hands as I' : belonging to the centuried pattern of 'Do it yourself, you're just as well able to as I am' or 'You can do it as easily as I can'.

'stand out of my spitting Place' : merely, Stand out of my light (or way).

Nev. Well, but Miss, don't be angry.

Miss. No, I was never angry in my Life, but once, and then no Body cared for it; so, I resolved never to be angry again.

Nev. Well; but if you'll tye it, you shall never know what I'll do for you.

Miss. So I suppose truly.

Nev. Well, but I'll make you a fine Present one of these Days.

Miss. Ay, when the Devil is blind, and his Eyes are not sore yet.

'when the Devil is blind . . . not sore yet' : never. Usually in the shorter form, *when the Devil is blind*; the latter half may possibly be Swift's addition. Obsolete, I think, by – or soon after – 1900.

Nev. No, Miss, I'll send it you To-morrow.

Miss. Well, well, To-morrow's a new Day : But I suppose, you mean To-morrow come never.

'To-morrow's a new Day' : a 16th–20th century proverb, with an Ancient Greek prototype; in the 20th, 'To-morrow's another day'. Apperson cites a 19th century variant, 'To-morrow is untouched'. Compare the Arabic 'With to-day there is to-morrow' (Selwyn Champion, *Racial Proverbs*, 1938).

'To-morrow come never' : 16th–20th centuries; by 1960, slightly archaic.

Nev. O, tis the prettiest Thing; I assure you there came but two of them over in three Ships.

'there came but two of them over in three Ships'. Tom, exercising his fancy, perhaps refers to a silk kerchief or handkerchief from the Orient.

Miss. Would I could see it, quoth blind *Hugh:* But, why did not you bring me a Present of Snuff this Morning?

'Would I could see it . . .' : a 16th–18th century proverb. A 17th century variant was '. . . blind George'. Compare the already noted 'A blind man would be glad to see that'.

Nev. Because, Miss, you never askt me; and 'tis an ill Dog that is not worth whistling for.

'an ill Dog . . . not worth whistling for' : semantically related perhaps to 'To a blind horse a nod is as good as a wink' and probably to 'It is an ill dog that deserves not a crust'.

Lord Sp. [*to Lady* Answerall.] Pray, Madam, how came your Ladyship last *Thursday* to go to that odious Puppet-Show?

Col. Why, to be sure her Ladyship went to see, and to be seen.

'her Ladyship went to see, and to be seen' : a proverbial phrase that probably derives from Ovid's *Spectatum veniunt, veniunt spectentur ut ipsae,* 'They' – the ladies – 'come to see; they come that they may themselves be seen' : compare the terse *visum visu* (to see and be seen). But wasn't Ovid forestalled by Theocritus?

Lady Ans. You have made a fine Speech, Colonel; pray, what will you take for your Mouthpiece?

'what will you take for your Mouthpiece?' : Who thought of it for you? Perhaps, however, as the *OED* assumes: humorous for 'mouth', as *headpiece* is for 'head'.

Lord Sp. Take that, Colonel. But, pray Madam, was my Lady *Dimple* there? They say she is extreamly handsome.

Lady Sm. They must not see with my Eyes that think so.

Nev. She may pass Muster, and that's all.

Lady Ans. Pray how old do you take her to be?

Col. Why, about five or six and twenty.

Miss. I swear she's no Chicken, she's on the wrong Side of thirty, if she be a Day.

> 'she's no Chicken': no longer young – a colloquialism as popular now as then. Also colloquialisms are 'on the wrong side of' and 'never see (a stated age)' – now with 'again' added.

Lady Ans. Depend upon't, she'll never see five and thirty, and a Bit to spare.

Col. Why they say, she's one of the chief Toasts in Town.

Lady Sm. Ay, when all the rest are out of it.

Miss. Well; I would not be as sick, as she's proud, for all the World.

Lady Ans. She looks as if Butter would not melt in her Mouth; but I warrant Cheese won't choak her.

> 'Butter would not melt in her Mouth': a proverb, applied also to men, of the 16th–20th centuries. The latter half ('Cheese won't choak her') belongs to the 17th–mid-19th centuries and implies that she will take a man.

Nev. I hear, my Lord what d'ye call 'um is courting her.

> 'what d'ye call 'um': what-do-you-call-him. Compare 'Lord of the Lord knows what', and Saintsbury's comment: 'A peerage revived with slightly altered title by Peter Simple's shipmates in favour of "the Lord Nozoo"' (Knows who) in Frederick Marryat's *Peter Simple*, 1834.

Lord Sp. What Lord d'ye mean, *Tom?*

Miss. Why, my Lord, I suppose, Mr. *Neverout* means the Lord of the Lord knows what.

Col. They say she dances very fine.

Lady Ans. She did; but I doubt her dancing Days are over.

Col. I can't pardon her for her rudeness to me.

Lady Sm. Well, but you must forget and forgive.

> 'forget and forgive': usually 'forgive and forget' – a phrase dating from the 12th century.

[Footman comes in.]

Lady Sm. Did you call *Betty?*

Footman. She's coming, Madam.

Lady Sm. Coming? Ay so is *Christmas.*

'Coming? Ay so is *Christmas*': an ironic saying of the 18th–20th centuries.

[Betty *comes in.*]

Lady Sm. Come, get ready my Things, where has the Wench been these three Hours?

Betty. Madam, I can't go faster than my Legs will carry me.

'can't go faster . . . carry me': apparently a catch-phrase of the period.

Lady Sm. Ay, thou hast a Head, and so has a Pin.——But, my Lord, all the Town has it, that Miss *Caper* is to be married to Sir *Peter Gibeall.* One Thing is certain, that she has promised to have him.

'thou hast a Head, and so has a Pin': a very small head; hence, no sense. Compare the late 19th–20th century *pin-head,* a noodle.

Lord Sp. Why, Madam, you know Promises are either broken or kept.

'Promises are either broken or kept': often preceded by 'all', this proverb belongs to the 16th–19th centuries but is rare after *c.* 1800.

Lady Ans. I beg your Pardon, my Lord, Promises and Pye-Crusts, they say, are made to be broken.

'Promises and Pye-Crusts . . .': mid-16th–20th centuries, but rare after *c.* 1900.

Lady Sm. Nay, I had it from my Lady *Carrilye's* own Mouth; I tell my Tale, and my Tale's Author; if it be a Lye, you had it as cheap as I.

'I tell my Tale, and my Tale's Author': I'm not making it up: late 17th–18th centuries.

'If it be a Lye . . . as I': another jingle of the kind fashionable early in the 18th century.

Lady Ans. She and I had some Words last *Sunday* at Church; but I think I gave her her own.

'had some Words': quarrelled. To *have words* occurs as early as the 15th century and does not become colloquial until *c.* 1700, nor common until much later; in the 20th century, regarded as proletarian.

'gave her her own': gave her as good as I got; held my own with her.

Lady Sm. Her Tongue runs like the Clapper of a Mill; she talks enough for her self and all the Company.

> 'Her Tongue runs like the Clapper of a Mill' : she talks too much and too loudly. Obsolete by 1850 at latest. – The clapper is that contrivance which causes the grain to descend to the mill-stones.

Nev. And yet she simpers like a Furmity Kettle.

> 'simpers like a Furmity Kettle' : like a pot of furmety (or, usually, frumenty) – hulled wheat boiled in milk : 16th–18th centuries. With an allusion to the now only dialectal *simper,* to simmer.

Miss. [*Looking in a Glass.*] Lord, how my Head is drest to Day!
Col. O Madam, a good Face needs no Band.

> 'a good Face needs no Band' : band = broad ribbon : 17th–18th centuries. Miss Notable's complement is probably her own.

Miss. No, and a bad one deserves none.
Col. Pray, Miss, where is your old Acquaintance Mrs. *Wayward?*
Miss. Why where should she be? If you must needs know; she's in her Skin.

> 'she's in her Skin' : a catch-phrase still heard occasionally. The Colonel's remark, ending with 'in', forms a crambo.

Col. I can answer that : What if you were as far out, as she's in?
Miss. Well, I promised to go this Evening to *Hide-Park* on the *Water; but, I protest, I'm half afraid.
Nev. Miss, Never fear : You have the old Proverb on your Side; naught's never in Danger.

> 'naught's never in Danger' : 17th–20th century, but, in the 19th– 20th, mostly rural : 'a proverb used when a worthless person is prosperous, or a worthless thing escapes destruction' (cited, by Apperson, from an 1889 glossarist).

Col. Why, Miss, let *Tom Neverout* wait on you, and then I warrant you will be as safe as a Thief in a Mill; for you know, he that is born to be hang'd, will never be drown'd.

> 'as safe as a Thief in a Mill' : same period and status. Very safe.
> 'he that is born . . . drown'd' : late 16th–20th centuries.

Nev. Thank ye, Colonel, for your good Word; but faith, if ever I hang, it shall be about a fair Lady's Neck.

> 'your good Word' : your kind remark.

Lady Sm. Who's there? Bid the Children be quiet, and not laugh so loud.

---

* *A Cant Phrase for taking Pleasure on the River* Thames *in a boat.*

Lady Ans. O, Madam, let 'em laugh; they'll ne'er laugh younger.

> 'they'll ne'er laugh younger' : If the children cannot laugh freely now, when *will* they be able to do so?

Nev. Miss, I'll tell you a Secret, if you'll promise never to tell it again.

Miss. No, to be sure, I'll tell it to no Body but Friends and Strangers.

> 'I'll tell it . . . Strangers' : tell it to everyone. Apparently a catch-phrase.

Nev. Why then, here's some Dirt in my Tea-Cup.

Miss. Come, come; the more there's in't, the more there's on't.

> 'The more there's in't . . .' : a lost saying – perhaps a proverb, perhaps a catch-phrase.

Lady Ans. Poh, you must eat a Peck of Dirt before you dye.

> 'eat a Peck of Dirt before you dye' : with variants of 'you', this proverb goes back to *c.* 1600. The 19th century added, 'but none of us wants it all at once'.

Col. Ay, ay, it all goes one Way.

> 'it all goes one way' : a proverbial saying, with variant 'the one way'. Extant.

Nev. Pray Miss, what's o' Clock?

Miss. Why, you must know 'tis a Thing like a Bell; and you're a Fool that can't tell.

> 'Why, you must know . . . tell' : a jingle.

Nev. [*to Lady* Answ.] Pray Madam do you tell me, for I let my Watch run down.

Lady Answ. Why, 'tis half an Hour past Hanging Time.

> '. . . past Hanging Time' : a catch-phrase, with varying duration. Now rare.

Col. Well; I am like the Butcher, that was looking for his Knife, and had it in his Mouth: I have been searching my Pockets for my Snuff-Box, and, I gad, here it is in my Hand.

> 'like the Butcher . . . Mouth' : 17th–18th (? early 19th) centuries; several slight variations.

Miss. If it had been a Bear, 'twould have bit you, Colonel: Well, I wish I had such a Snuff-Box.

> 'if it had been a Bear . . .' : also, 'if it were a bear, it would bite you' : 17th–18th centuries. Has lingered on, with variant 'dog'.

Nev. You'll be long enough before you wish your Skin full of Eyelet-Holes.

> 'Skin full of Eyelet-Holes' (dead) : 16th–18th centuries.

Col. Wish in one Hand————

> 'Wish in one Hand—' : Miss gives herself away by the haste with which she interrupts the Colonel. Clearly she knows how the scabrous proverb ends.

Miss. Out upon you; Lord, what can the Man mean?

Lord Sp. This Tea's very hot?

Lady Answ. Why, it came from a hot Place my Lord.

> 'it came from a hot Place' (comment upon 'This tea's very hot') : a catch-phrase – variant 'comes' – still current, although perhaps rather less after than before *c.* 1940.

> *[Colonel spills his Tea.]*

Lady Sm. That's as well done, as if I had done it my self.

> '[*Colonel spills his Tea*] *Lady Sm.* That's as well done ... myself' : a catch-phrase, now often in form 'I could do as well myself' or 'I could have done it ...' or 'I couldn't have done it better myself'.

Col. Madam, I find you live by ill Neighbours, when you are forced to praise your self.

> 'live by ill Neighbours ...' : a 15th–18th (? also 19th) century proverb, with variants 'dwell by' or 'have' and usually in the third person.

Nev. Well; I won't drink a Drop more: If I do, 'twill go down like chopt Hay.

> 'go down like chopt Hay' (will taste like it) : 17th–18th century proverbial phrase.

Miss. Pray don't you say no 'till you are ask'd.

> 'don't you say no ...' (you haven't been asked) : a catch-phrase, extant in any of several forms.

Nev. Well; what you please, and the rest again.

> 'what you please, and the rest again' : perhaps = Oh, well, have it your own way!

Miss. [*stooping for a Pin.*] I have heard 'em say, a Pin a-Day, is a Groat a Year. Well, as I hope to be married (forgive me for Swearing) I vow it is a Needle.

> 'a Pin a-day ...' : an 18th–19th century proverb, latterly rural.
> 'forgive me for Swearing' : a humorous catch-phrase = if I may mention it.

Col. O the wonderful Works of Nature! that a black Hen should have a white Egg.

'a black Hen . . . a white Egg' : ironic. 'Pin or needle – what does it matter?'

Nev. What; you have found a Mare's Nest and laugh at the Eggs.

'found a Mare's nest . . . Eggs' : in 16th–17th centuries, *find a mare's nest*; in 18th–20th (19th–20th : rural), as in Swift; in 19th–20th, also the allusive *a mare's nest,* an illusory, or a trivial, discovery.

Miss. Pray keep your Breath to cool your Porridge.

'keep your Breath . . . Porridge' : 16th–20th centuries, with variants 'save' and 'wind' and 'broth'. Don't waste your time in talking.

Nev. Miss there was a very pleasant Accident last Night in St. *James's-Park.*

'Accident' : episode.

Miss. [*to Lady* Smart.] What was it your Ladyship was going to say just now?

Nev. Well Miss; tell a Mare a Tale————

'tell a Mare a Tale—' : the 16th–17th (and presumably the Swiftian) completion is 'and she'll gerd out' – deliver – 'a fart'. (Apperson.) Miss would again seem to know the proverb.

Miss. I find you love to hear yourself talk.

Nev. Why, if you won't hear my Tale, kiss my, &c.

'kiss my, &c.' : '&c.' (*et cetera*) is a euphemism merely scriptural, for clearly Tom Neverout says 'arse'.

Miss. Out upon you for a filthy Creater.

'Creater' : a late 17th–18th century pronunciation (*creé-ter*) of *creature.*

Nev. What, Miss; must I tell you a Story and find you Ears?

'tell you a Story . . . ears' : a 16th–18th century proverbial saying; usually 'tale'.

Lord Sp. [*to Lady* Smart.] Pray Madam, don't you think Mrs. *Spendal* very genteel?

Lady Sm. Why, my Lord, I think she was cut out for a Gentlewoman, but she was spoiled in the making. She wears her Cloaths as if they were thrown on with a Pitch-Fork; and, for the Fashion, I believe they were made in the Days of Queen *Bess.*

'cut out for a Gentlewoman, but . . . spoiled in the making' : it follows the pattern, *cut out for a* [something or other], *but spoiled in the making.*

'wears her Cloaths . . . thrown on with a Pitch-Fork' : one of many such phrases condemning clothes badly worn. Perhaps the wittiest phrase I've heard is the post-1945 'tailored by Vickers-Armstrong'.

'made in the Days of Queen *Bess*' : compare 'Queen *Elizabeth's* dead' on the third page of this Dialogue.

Nev. Well, that's neither here nor there; for, you know the more careless, the more modish.

'neither here nor there' (immaterial) goes back to the 16th century. 'the more careless, the more modish' : the better one's clothes, the more carelessly one wears them.

Col. Well, I'd hold a Wager there will be a Match between her and *Dick Dolt;* and I believe I can see as far into a Millstone as another Man.

'see as far . . . as another Man' : 16th–18th centuries; then mostly 'see through a brick wall'. Where nothing is known – where all is in doubt – my opinion's as good as the next man's.

Miss. Colonel, I must beg your Pardon a thousand Times, but they say, an old Ape has an old Eye.

'an old Ape . . .' : late 16th–18th centuries.

Nev. Miss, what do you mean? you'll spoil the Colonel's Marriage if you call him old.

Col. Not so old nor yet so cold————You know the rest Miss.

'Not so old nor yet so cold – You know the rest Miss' : Apperson has *not so old* and quotes Swift and adds, 'I hope "Miss" did know the rest – I do not'; *ODEP* ignores Swift but, at *old and cold*, cites J. Kelly's *Scotish Proverbs*, 1721, thus : '*He is old and cold, and ill to lye beside.* Spoken by a young maid, when jeer'd' – *geared*, provided, equipped – 'with an old man'. Therefore Swift's version ends with some such words as 'that I cannot keep a maid warm'.

Miss. Manners is a fine Thing truly.

Col. Faith Miss, depend upon it, I'll give you as good as you bring. What? if you give a Jest, you must take a Jest.

'if you give a Jest . . .' : you must learn to take a joke if you make a joke.

Lady Sm. Well, Mr. *Neverout*, you'll never have done 'till you break that Knife, and then the Man won't take it again.

Miss. Why Madam, Fools will be meddling; I wish he may cut his Fingers: I hope, you can see your own Blood without fainting?

> 'Fools will be meddling': prototyped in the 14th century, established by The Bible in 1611 ('Every fool will be meddling'), common in the 18th–mid-19th century (Apperson and *ODEP*).

Nev. Why, Miss you shine this Morning like a sh——Barn-Door; you'll never hold out at this Rate; pray save a little Wit for To-morrow.

> 'shine . . . like a sh— Barn-Door': Neverout of course says 'shitten': a proverbial saying of late 17th–mid-19th century. Recorded also by Francis Grose in his *Vulgar Tongue* (3rd edition).

Miss. Well, you have said your Say: If People will be rude, I have done. My Comfort is, it will be all one a thousand Years hence.

> 'it will be all one . . .': a variation of the theme 'It'll all be one' – or 'the same' – 'a hundred years hence' or 'in a hundred years': probably since *c.* 1550.

Nev. Miss, and you have shot your Bolt: I find you must have the last Word: Well, I'll go to the Opera to Night.——No, I can't neither, for I have some Business——and yet I think I must; for I promised to squire the Countess to her Box.

Miss. The Countess of *Puddledock* I suppose.

> 'Countess of Puddledock': the feminine of 'Lord of the Lord Knows what' (noted earlier in this Dialogue) or the 19th–20th century proletarian 'Lord Muck'.

Nev. Peace or War, Miss?

Lady Sm. Well, Mr Neverout you'll never be mad, you are of so many Minds.

> 'never be mad . . . of so many Minds': a 16th–18th (? early 19th) century proverb based on very sound psychology: to go mad, one must have a mind to go mad *with*.

[*As Miss rises, the Chair falls behind her.*]

Miss. Well, I shan't be Lady Mayoress this Year.

Nev. No, Miss, 'tis worse than that, you won't be married this Year.

> '[*As Miss rises, the Chair falls . . .*] . . . shan't be Lady Mayoress . . . 'you won't be married this year': two unrelated pieces of folk-lore here brought together for effect. The former is obsolete; the second, still heard occasionally among those who cling to such things.

Miss. Lord! you make me laugh though I a'n't well.

'a'n't' : a late 17th–19th century colloquial and 20th century illiterate (when not dialectal) form of 'am not'. – For 'is not', it has always been either dialectal or illiterate.

[Neverout *as Miss is standing pulls her suddenly on his Lap.*]

Nev. Colonel, come sit down on my Lap; more Sacks on the Mill.

'more Sacks on the Mill' (usually '. . . to . . .') : 16th–20th centuries, but, since *c.* 1800, mostly rural. The proverb originated, rather than originated in, a boisterous game. (Apperson.)

Miss. Let me go : An't you sorry for my Heaviness?

Nev. No Miss; you are very light, but I don't say, You are a light Hussy. Pray take up the Chair for your Pains.

'a light Hussy' : a wanton.

Miss. 'Tis but one Body's Labour, you may do it your self. I wish you would be quiet, you have more Tricks than a dancing Bear.

'more Tricks than a dancing Bear' : recorded by Ray in 1670; obsolete by 1850 at the latest. The 20th century has 'as full of tricks as a bagful of monkeys'; compare the late 19th–20th century 'monkey-tricks', sexual liberties.

[Neverout *rises to take up the Chair, and Miss sits in his.*]

Nev. You would not be so soon in my Grave, Madam.

'so soon in my Grave' : perhaps a catch-phrase of the period.

Miss. Lord, I have torn my Pettycoat with your odious romping; my Rents are coming in; I'm afraid I shall fall into the Ragman's Hands.

'my Rents are coming in' and 'fall into the Ragman's Hands' : *rents* in one's clothing lead to old clothes falling into the hands of the *ragman* or old-clothes-man (who buys them and sells them). These are catch-phrases, not proverbs.

Nev. I'll mend it, Miss.

Miss. You mend it ! Go teach your Grannum to suck Eggs.

'teach your Grannum . . .' : with such variations as 'to spin' and 'to sup milk', this proverb goes back to the early 16th century.

Nev. Why, Miss, you are so cross, I could find in my Heart to hate you.

Miss. With all my Heart; I can assure you, there will be no Love lost between us.

'no Love lost between us' : no affection for each other. Whereas this sense, originating in the 17th century, is extant, the contrasting sense 'a mutual love', originating at the same period, has been obsolete since *c.* 1850.

Nev. But, pray my Lady *Smart,* does not Miss look as if she could eat me without Salt?

'could eat me without Salt' : finds me so delightful that she could eat me. Perhaps a catch-phrase. Compare the 19th–20th century 'good enough to eat'.

Miss. I'll make you one Day sup Sorrow for this.

'sup Sorrow' : be very sorry. A 14th–18th century metaphor.

Nev. Well, follow your own Way, you'll live the longer.

'follow your own Way . . . longer' : perhaps a catch-phrase.

Miss. See, Madam, how well I have mended it.
Lady Sm. 'Tis indifferent, as *Doll* danc'd.

' 'Tis indifferent, as *Doll* danc'd' : probably another.

Nev. 'Twill last as many Nights as Days.

'last as many Nights as Days' : for a (short) while. A catch-phrase.

Miss. Well, I knew I should never have your good Word.
Lady Sm. My Lord; Lady *Answerall* and I, were walking in the Park last Night till near Eleven; 'twas a very fine Night.
Nev. I'gad so was I, and I'll tell you a comical Accident. I'gad I lost my Understanding.

'lost my Understanding' : by a pun, he means his shoe. Slang uses *understandings* both for 'boots or shoes' and derivatively for 'legs'; Miss pretends to misunderstand. Perhaps compare the proverb (cited by *ODEP*) : 'Who has not understanding, let him have legs'.

Miss. I'm glad you had any to lose.
Lady Sm. Well, but what do you mean?
Nev. I'gad I kickt my Feet against a Stone, and tore off the Heel of my Shoe, and was forced to limp to a Cobler in the *Pellmell,* to have it put on. He, he, he. [*All laugh.*]

'the *Pellmell*' : Pall Mall.

Col. O, 'twas a delicate Night to run away with another Man's Wife.

'delicate Night . . . Wife' : a late 16th–18th century proverbial saying, mostly with 'fine' for 'delicate'. A moonlit night.

[Neverout *sneezes.*]

Miss. God bless you, if you have not taken Snuff.

'God bless you' : a 16th–20th century proverbial saying. Now simply 'Bless you !'

Nev. Why, what if I have, Miss?

87

Miss. Why then the Duce take you.

'the Duce take you' : the Deuce, or Devil, take you! Obsolete.

Nev. Miss, I want that Diamond Ring of Yours.

Miss. Why then, Want's like to be your Master.

'Want's like to be your Master' : You'll just have to go on wanting. (18th century only.) Also 'Want will be your master' : 19th–20th century.

[Neverout *looking at the Ring.*]

Nev. Ay marry, this is not only, but also; pray, where did you get it?

'This is not only, but also' : either 'This is too much!' or, of the ring, 'not only handsome but valuable' or some such ellipsis.

Miss. Why, where it was to be had; where the Devil got the Fryar.

'where it was to be had' : a 'catch' reply, reinforced by 'where the Devil got the Fryar' – where do you think? Explained by 'Where the devil had the friar, but where was he?' (Davenport, 1639) – wherever it happened to be. (Apperson.)

Nev. Well, if I had such a fine Diamond Ring, I would not stay a Day in *England*. But you know, far fetch'd and dear bought, is fit for Ladies. I warrant this cost your Father two Pence half Penny.

'far fetch'd and dear bought' : a 14th–20th century, since *c.* 1920, obsolescent, dictum of which the full form is 'Dear bought and far-fetched' – or the other way about – 'are dainties' – or 'good' – 'for ladies'. (See especially *ODEP*.)

'cost . . . two Pence half Penny' : compare the 19th–20th century 'some *twopenny-ha'penny* thing'.

[*Miss sitting between* Neverout *and the Colonel.*]

Miss. Well, here's a Rose between two Nettles.

'a Rose between two Nettles' : now 'a rose between two thorns' (a girl – especially 'an English *Rose*' – between two men.

Nev. No, Madam, with Submission, there's a Nettle between two Roses.

[*Colonel stretching himself.*]

Lady Sm. Why, Colonel, you break the King's Laws, you stretch without a Halter.

'you break the King's Laws . . . Halter' : probably a catch-phrase rather than (*pace ODEP*) a proverbial saying.

Lady Answ. Colonel, some Ladies of your Acquaintance have promised to Breakfast with you, and I am to wait on them; what will you give us?

Col. Why, Faith Madam, Batchelor's Fare, Bread and Cheese, and Kisses.

> 'Batchelor's Fare . . .': although recorded only in Swift and in Grose's *Vulgar Tongue,* 3rd edition, 1796, the saying is extant, although rarely heard since *c.* 1940.

Lady Answ. Poh, what have you Batchelors to do with your Money, but to treat the Ladies? You have nothing to keep but your own four Quarters.

> 'your own four Quarters': lodgings. A pun on *quarters,* lodgings, and 'the *four quarters* of the globe'.

Lady Answ. My Lord; has Captain *Strut* the Honour to be related to your Lordship?

Lord Sp. Very nearly, Madam; he's my Cousin German quite removed.

> 'Cousin German quite removed': no relation at all, a *cousin-german* (germane) being already a first cousin once removed.

Lady Answ. Pray is not he rich?

Lord Sp. Ay, a rich Rogue, two Shirts and a Rag.

> 'a rich Rogue, two Shirts and a Rag': a thorough rogue, but almost penniless. Recorded in Ray's *Proverbs,* 1678, but apparently obsolete by *c.* 1800.

Col. Well; however they say he has a great Estate, but only the right Owner keeps him out of it.

> 'great Estate . . . out of it': in Ray, 1678, the proverb runs, 'He has a good taste, but that the right owner keeps it from him': he has pretensions but no just claim.

Lady Sm. What Religion is he of?

Lord Sp. Why; he is an Anythingarian.

> 'an Anythingarian': Tom Brown used it in 1704; obsolescent. A sense-exaggeration and a form-imitation of *Latitudinarian,* a person, especially a cleric, broad-minded in religious matters, coined *c.* 1670.

Lady Answ. I believe, he has his Religion to chuse, my Lord.

[*Neverout scratches his Neck.*]

Miss. Fye, Mr. *Neverout,* an't you ashamed? I beg Pardon for the Expression; but I'm afraid your Bosom Friends are become your Backbiters.

Nev. Well, Miss, I saw a Flea once on your Pinner; and a Louse is a Man's Companion, but a Flea is a Dog's Companion. However, I wish you would scratch my Neck with your pretty white Hand.

'your Bosom Friends . . .': lice have moved from chest to back.
Compare 'No friend like to a bosom friend, as the man said who
pulled out a louse' recorded by Thomas Fuller in 1732. In the First
World War, British soldiers spoke of 'bosom chums', a term that,
during the Second World War, I heard in neither the Army nor the
RAF.

'a Louse . . . , but a Flea . . .': on the other hand, a 16th–17th
century proverb rightly asserts that 'a louse is a beggar's companion'.

Miss. And who would be Fool then? I would not touch a Man's
Flesh for the Universe: You have the wrong Sow by the Ear; I
assure you that's Meat for your Master.

'have the wrong Sow by the Ear': are addressing the wrong
person: 16th–20th centuries, but rarely heard in the 20th.

'Meat for your Master': 16th–19th centuries. Compare Shakespeare's 'I am meat, etc.' (1598.)

Col. Well, I must be plain, here's a very bad Smell.

Miss. Perhaps, Colonel, the Fox is the finder.

'the Fox is the finder': the complainant is, in truth, the guilty
party: late 17th–19th centuries, with variant 'The fox smells his
own stink first'.

Nev. No, Colonel, 'tis only your Teeth against Rain. But,

'your Teeth against Rain': perhaps 'your word against hers'.

Miss. Colonel, I find, you would make a very good poor Man's Sow.
But,

'poor Man's Sow': 16th–18th centuries, usually 'to have a good
nose to be' – or 'make' – 'a poor man's sow', as indeed in Dialogue III. Exact sense?

Nev. Miss *Notable;* all Quarrels laid aside, pray step hither for a
Moment.

Miss. I'll wash my Hands and wait on you, Sir; but pray come you
hither, and try to open this Lock.

Nev. We'll try what we can do.

Miss. We! what, have you Pigs in your Belly?

'have you Pigs . . . ?': a comment on the rather pompous use of
the plural 'we'.

Nev. I assure you, Miss, I am very handy at all Things.

Miss. Marry hang them, that can't give themselves a good Word, I
believe you may have an even Hand to throw a Louse into the Fire.

'have an even Hand . . .': have a hand steady enough to . . .

[Colonel coughing.]

Col. I have got a sad Cold.

'sad cold' : a serious one.

Lady Answ. Ay, 'tis well if one can get any Thing these hard Times.

'these hard Times' : one seems to have heard this somewhere.

Miss. [*To Colonel.*] Choak Chicken, there's another a Hatching.

'Choak Chicken . . . Hatching' : 16th (and probably earlier)–20th centuries. Ray's version, 1678, is 'Choak up, the churchyard's nigh'. Generic sense : There are plenty of other good men – there's always another coming along.

Lady Sm. Pray, Colonel, how did you get that Cold?

Lord Sp. Why, Madam, I suppose the Colonel got it by lying a-Bed barefoot.

'got it . . . barefoot' : the implication being that he is very delicate.

Lady Answ. Why, then Colonel, you must take it for better for worse, as a Man takes his Wife.

Col. Well, Ladies, I apprehend you without a Constable.

'apprehend you without a Constable' : a pun on the 'understand' and 'arrest' senses of *apprehend*. A smart catch-phrase of the period.

Miss. Mr. *Neverout*, Mr. *Neverout*, come hither this Moment.

Lady Sm. [*imitating her.*] Mr. *Neverout*, Mr. *Neverout*, I wish he were ty'd to your Girdle.

Nev. What's the Matter? Whose Mare's dead now?

'Whose Mare's dead now?' : What on earth is the matter? Usually 'Whose mare is dead?' – mid-16th–mid-19th centuries. A recent equivalent : 'Where's the fire?' – which, however, throws rather more emphasis on the element or aspect of urgency.

Miss. Take your Labour for your Pains, you may go back again like a Fool as you came.

'you may go back again . . . as you came' : an addition – either Swift's or fashionable at the time – to the proverbial 16th–19th century 'have nothing but one's labour for one's pains'; in the 18th–19th also 'trouble' instead of 'labour'.

Nev. Well, Miss, if you deceive me a second Time, it's my Fault.

Lady Sm. Colonel, methinks your Coat is too short.

Col. It will be long enough, before I get another, Madam.

'It will be long enough . . .' : I'll accustom myself to it before I need another.

Miss. Come, come, the Coat's a good Coat, and come of good Friends.

'come of good Friends' : ? given by a friend.

Nev. Ladies, you are mistaken in the Stuff : 'tis half Silk.

Col. Tom Neverout, you're a Fool, and that's your Fault.

'Fool, and that's your Fault' : you talk foolishly – and yet you're no fool.

[*A great Noise below.*]

Lady Sm. Hey, what a clattering is there; one would think Hell was broke loose.

'Hell was broke loose' (now, 'had broken loose') : dates from the 16th century; if not rather from a century or two earlier.

Miss. Indeed, Madam, I must take my Leave, for I an't well.

Lady Sm. What, you are sick of the Mulligrubs with eating chopt Hay.

'Mulligrubs' : stomach-ache. Like *collywobbles,* a jocularly arbitrary word : their base being *grubs* and *colic.* – 'chopt Hay' : for the second time.

Miss. No indeed, Madam, to say the Truth of it, I'm sick and hungry, more need of a Cook than a Doctor.

Lady Ans. Poor Miss, she's sick as a Cushion, she wants nothing but stuffing.

'sick as a Cushion' : not sick at all; merely hungry. Mid-17th–18th century.

Col. If you are sick, you shall have a Caudle of Calves Eggs.

'a Caudle of Calves Eggs' : a mythical remedy that did not, I think, become a proverbial phrase; it may have been a fashionable catch-phrase, with perhaps an allusion to the late 16th–17th century *caudle of hemp-seed* or its Shakespearean variant *hempen caudle.*

Nev. I can't find my Gloves.

Miss. I saw the Dog running away with some dirty Thing a while ago.

Col. Miss, you have got my Handkerchief; pray let me have it.

Lady Sm. No, keep it Miss, for they say Possession is eleven Points of the Law.

'Possession is eleven Points . . .' : the 17th–mid-19th century original of the 19th–20th century '. . . nine points of the law'. Eleven out of twelve; nine out of ten.

Miss. Madam, he shall never have it again; it is in Hucksters Hands.

'in Hucksters Hands' (hucksters'): beyond recovery. An idiomatic phrase of the mid-16th–18th centuries. (*OED.*)

Lady Answ. What; I see 'tis raining again.

Lord Sp. Why then, Madam, we must do as they do in *Spain*.

'as they do in *Spain* . . . we must let it rain': a crambo; but also in allusion to the 17th–20th 'Rain, rain, go to Spain, / Fair weather come again' (1659), whence the nursery rhyme.

Lady Sm. Pray, my Lord, how is that?

Lord Sp. Why, Madam, we must let it rain.

> [*Miss whispers Lady* Smart.]

Nev. Miss, there's no whispering but there's lying.

'there's no whispering . . .': in 1678, Ray cites the proverb in the form 'Where there is whispering there is lying': 17th–19th centuries.

Miss. Lord! Mr. *Neverout,* you are grown as pert as a Pearmonger this Morning.

'as pert as a Pearmonger': recorded first in 1564, it became, *c.* 1800, mainly rural. The variant (now dialectal) *peart* appears in the 17th–20th century, mainly Devonian, 'as peart as a sparrow'; the 19th–20th Lancashire-Yorkshire 'as peart as a robin'; and the Oxfordshire 'as peart as a maggot'. 'As pert as a pearmonger' has the semantic variant, 'as pert as a pearmonger's mare' (Ray, 1678). As a costardmonger (costermonger) sells costard apples, so a pearmonger . . . Here, *pert*=lively.

Nev. Indeed, Miss, you are very handsome.

Miss. Poh, I know that already, tell me News.

'tell me News': 17th–mid-19th century; then, 'Tell me something new'.

> [*Some Body knocks at the Door.*]
> [*Footman comes in.*]

Footman. [*to Col.*] An please your Honour, there's a Man below wants to speak to you.

Col. Ladies, your Pardon for a Minute.

> [*Colonel goes out.*]

Lady Sm. Miss, I sent Yesterday to know how you did, but you were gone abroad early.

'gone abroad': left your home (or lodgings), whether to shop or to visit.

Miss. Why, Madam, I was huncht up in a Hackney Coach with

three Country Acquaintance, who called upon me to take the Air as far as *Highgate*.

> 'take the Air as far as *Highgate*': at that time, Highgate was still a fashionable suburb on the northern outskirts of London.

Lady Sm. And had you a pleasant Airing?

Miss. No, Madam, it rain'd all the Time: I was jolted to Death, and the Road was so bad, that I screamed every Moment, and call'd to the Coachman, pray Friend don't spill us.

Nev. So, Miss, you were afraid that Pride should have a Fall.

> 'Pride should have a Fall': a syntactic alteration of 'Pride shall (*or* will) have a fall': 16th–20th centuries; anticipated in many moral writings.

Miss. Mr. *Neverout*, when I want a Fool, I'll send for you.

> 'when I want a Fool . . . you': compare the 17th century proverb, 'He that sends a fool, expects one'.

Lord Sp. Miss, did not your left Ear burn last Night?

> 'Did not your left Ear . . . ?': a 17th–20th century development from the 14th–16th century 'If your ears glow (*or* 'ear glows'), someone is talking of you'.

Miss. Pray why, my Lord?

Lord Sp. Because I was then in some Company, where you were extolled to the Skies, I assure you.

Miss. My Lord, that was more their Goodness, than my Desert.

> 'more their Goodness . . .': a conventionally modest reply – certainly not a catch-phrase and probably not a proverbial saying. Now: 'They are (much) too kind'.

Lord Sp. They said you were a compleat Beauty.

Miss. My Lord, I am as God made me.

> 'as God made me': by *ODEP* accounted a proverbial saying, as it almost certainly is – and has been since perhaps the 16th century. Compare 'But by the grace of God I am what I am' (1st *Corinthians*, xv, 8).

Lady Sm. The Girl's well enough if she had but another Nose.

> 'but another Nose': for instance, Cleopatra's. Miss replies with delightful irony.

Miss. O, Madam, I know I shall always have your good Word; you love to help a lame Dog over the Style.

> 'help a lame Dog . . .': a 16th–20th century proverbial phrase. More often 'a stile' than 'the stile'. Swift's *style* was idiosyncratic, not conventional.

[One knocks.]

Lady Sm. Who's there? You're on the wrong Side of the Door; come in if you be fat.

> 'come in if you be fat' : an 18th–19th century catch-phrase. On the assumption that a fat person is jolly and merry?

[Colonel comes in again.]

Lord Sp. Why, Colonel, you are a Man of great Business.

Col. Ay, my Lord; I'm like my Lord Mayor's Fool; full of Business and nothing to do.

> 'like my Lord Mayor's Fool . . . nothing to do' : an 18th century proverbial saying. Compare the 20th century's catch-phrase, 'all dressed up and nowhere to go'.

Lady Sm. My Lord, don't you think the Colonel's mightily fallen away of late?

Lord Sp. Ay, fallen from a Horse Load to a Cart-Load.

> 'fallen away . . . Ay, fallen . . . to a Cart-Load' : Yes, indeed; *much* stouter. Recorded in Ray, 1678, and applied especially to a sudden increase in weight.

Col. Why, my Lord, I'gad I am like a Rabbit, fat and lean in four and twenty Hours.

> 'like a Rabbit, fat and lean . . .' : also in Ray, 1678.

Lady Sm. I assure you, the Colonel walks as strait as a Pin.

> 'as strait as a Pin' : as straight as one, the *strait* spelling being very common. A variant of the very much more general '. . . as an arrow'.

Miss. Yes, he's a handsome bodied Man in the Face.

> 'a handsome bodied man in the Face' : well-made, but not good-looking. Ray, 1678.

Nev. A handsome Foot and Leg, God-a-Mercy Shoe and Stocking.

> 'God-a-Mercy' : God have mercy on (his shoes and stockings, so large are his legs and feet).

Col. What? three upon one, that's foul play. This would make a Parson swear.

> 'would make a Parson swear' : is most provoking. A colloquial variant of 'Enough to make a saint swear' (16th–20th centuries).

Nev. Why Miss; what's the Matter? You look as if you had neither won nor lost.

> 'look as if . . . neither won nor lost' : 16th–20th centuries, but after *c.* 1800 mostly rural.

Col. Why, you must know, Miss lives upon Love.

Miss. Yes, upon Love and Lumps of the Cupboard.

'Lumps of the Cupboard' : large portions from it. Compare 'Love and Pease-porridge'.

Lady Ans. Ay, they say Love and Pease-porridge are two dangerous Things; one breaks the Heart, and t'other the Belly.

'Love and Pease-porridge . . . the Belly' : in 1674, Head and Kirkman, *The English Rogue,* refer to it as 'the old proverb'; rare after *c.* 1850.

[Miss imitating Lady Answerall's Tone.]

Miss. Very pretty, one breaks the Heart, and t'other the Belly.

Lady Ans. Have a Care, Miss, they say mocking is catching.

'mocking is catching' : a 16th–20th century proverb. The mocker shall be mocked.

Miss. I never heard that.

Nev. Why then, Miss, you have one wrinkle – more than ever you had before.

'one more wrinkle' : one more useful little piece of knowledge. A pun and a compliment.

Miss. Well; live and learn.

'live and learn' : originally, Live to learn, but usually apprehended as Learn by living – that is, by experience. Since the 16th century. Neverout's addition may have been a smart catch-phrase elaboration.

Nev. Ay, and be hang'd, and forget all.

Miss. Well, Mr. Neverout, take it as you please; but I swear, you're a sawcy Jack for using such Expressions.

'a sawcy Jack' : an impudent fellow. *Jack* implied ill-breeding and bad manners.

Nev. Why then, Miss, if you go to that, I must tell you, that there's never a Jack, but there's a Jill.

'never a Jack . . . Jill' : 'Every Jack has' – or 'shall have' – 'his Jill' : 17th–20th centuries.

Miss. O, Mr. *Neverout,* every one knows that you are the Pink of Courtesy.

Nev. And, Miss, all the World allows that you are the Flower of Civility.

'the Pink of Courtesy' and 'the Flower of Civility' : compare Shakespeare's 'the very pink of courtesy' and 'the flower of courtesy' (*Romeo and Juliet,* II, iv, 61 and 44).

Lady Sm. Miss, I hear there was a great deal of Company where you visited last Night: Pray who were they?

Miss. Why, there was Lady *Forward*, Miss *Toandagain*, Sir *John Ogle*, my Lady *Clapper*; and I, quoth the Dog.

> 'and I, quoth the Dog': and my humble self. Compare the 'and friend' of Society photographs and news-items, e.g. 'Lord X. and friend'. Compare also: 'poor Pillgarlick'.

Col. Was your Visit long, Miss?

Miss. Why truly, they went all to the Opera, and so poor Pillgarlick came home alone.

> 'poor Pillgarlick': myself. Usually 'Pilgarlic' *solus*: 'originally a bald head, but became a proverbial name for any unlucky wight, sometimes in self-application' (Apperson): 16th–mid-18th century, then literary or allusive. A *pilled* or peeled head of garlic.

Nev. Alack a Day, poor Miss, methinks it grieves me to pity you.

Miss. What, you think you said a fine Thing now; well, if I had a Dog with no more Wit, I would hang him.

> 'if I had a Dog . . . hang him': probably a catch-phrase of the period.

Lady Sm. Miss, if it be Manners, may I ask which is oldest, you, or Lady *Scuttle?*

Miss. Why, my Lord, when I dye for Age, she may quake for Fear.

> 'when I dye for Age . . .': When I die of old age, she will quake for fear – if she's not already dead. Implication: the other isn't much younger. Very common in the 18th century.

Lady Sm. She's a very great Gadder abroad.

Lady Sm. Lord! she made me follow her last Week through all the Shops like a Tantiny Pig.

> 'a Tantiny Pig': usually '*Tantony* pig' for 'St *Anthony*'s pig'; also, in Stow's *Survey of London*, 1598, 'an Anthonie pig'. St. Anthony, the patron saint of swineherds, has pigs under his protection – they were formerly allowed to roam unmolested, following whom they would. (*ODEP*.) In the conventional pictures, St Anthony usually has a pig as companion.

Lady Sm. I remember you told me, you had been with her from *Dan* to *Bersheba.*

> 'from *Dan* to *Bersheba*': 'from Dan even to Beer-sheba' (*Judges*, xx, 1) – from north to south of ancient Palestine; hence, throughout the region; hence, everywhere.

Miss. O, Mr. *Neverout,* my little *Countess* has just littered; speak me fair, and I'll set you down for a Puppy.

Nev. Why Miss, if I speak you fair, perhaps I mayn't tell Truth.

Lord Sp. Ay, but *Tom,* smoak that, she calls you Puppy by Craft.

'smoak that': 'Get that!' – Understand the point she's making!

Nev. Well, Miss, you ride the fore horse To-Day.

'you ride the fore horse': you are in front of me, forestall me, outwit me. A proverbial saying of mid-17th–mid-19th century.

Miss. Ay, many a one says well, that thinks ill.

'many a one says well . . .': contrast the 17th century proverb, 'Many speak much who cannot speak well.'

Nev. Fye, Miss, you said that once before; and you know, too much of one Thing is good for nothing.

'too much of one Thing . . .': a 16th–19th century proverb.

Miss. Why sure, one can't say a good Thing too often.

'one can't say a good Thing too often': Shakespeare, *As You Like It* (IV, i, 128), 'Why then, can one desire too much of a good thing?'

Lord Sp. Well; so much for that, and Butter for Fish. Let us call another Cause. Pray, Madam, does your Ladyship know Mrs. *Nice?*

'so much for that, and Butter for Fish': also 'That is for that, and butter's for fish' (recorded in 1721).

'call another Cause': deal with – especially, talk about – something else. From legal *cause,* a case in the courts.

Lady Sm. Perfectly well, my Lord; she is nice by Name, and nice by Nature.

'nice by Name . . .': compare the 17th–19th century proverb with a Biblical adumbration – 'Names and natures do often agree'. Here, *nice* = fastidious.

Lord Sp. Is it possible that she could take that Booby *Tom Blunder* for Love?

Miss. She had good Skill in Horse Flesh, that could chuse a Goose to ride on.

'good Skill in Horse Flesh . . .': an ironic proverb, recorded by Ray, 1670, thus, 'He hath good skill in horseflesh, to buy a goose to ride on'.

Lady Answ. Why, my Lord, it was her Fate; they say Marriage and hanging go by Destiny.

'Marriage and hanging . . .': a 16th–19th century proverb, often in form – 'Hanging and wiving (*or* wedding) go by destiny'.

Col. I believe, she'll never be burnt for a Witch.

'she'll never be burnt . . .': a variant of the 17th–mid-19th century proverb, 'They that burn you (*or* them *or* . . .) for a witch, will lose their coals (and labour)'. Kelly, 1721, explains as 'no conjurer'; perhaps rather, 'no enchantress'.

Lord Sp. They say Marriages are made in Heaven; but I doubt when she was marry'd she had no Friends there.

'Marriages are made in Heaven': 16th–20th centuries. Apperson compares 'A prudent wife is from the Lord' (the Biblical *Proverbs,* xix, 14).

Nev. Well, she's got out of God's Blessing into the warm Sun.

'got out of God's Blessing into the warm Sun': changed from better to worse: 16th–20th centuries, although not much heard since *c.* 1940.

Col. The Fellow's well enough, if he had any Guts in his Brains.

'had any Guts in his Brains' (had any sense): 17th–20th centuries; since *c.* 1800, mostly rural.

Lady Sm. They say, thereby hangs a Tale.

'thereby hangs a Tale': the slightly earlier 'Thereby lieth a tale' yielded to this, which is Shakespeare's, form – he uses it at least thrice; the example in *Othello,* III, i, shows that he was well aware of the pun on *tale* – *tail.*

Lord Sp. Why, he's a meer Hobbledehoy, neither Man nor Boy.

'Hobbledehoy, neither Man nor Boy': a proverbial phrase, apparently recorded first – rather than coined – by Palsgrave, 1540 (Apperson). For *hobbledehoy,* see my *Origins.*

Miss. Well, if I were to chuse a Husband, I would never be marry'd to a little Man.

Nev. Pray why so, Miss? For they say of all Evils we ought to chuse the least.

'of all Evils . . . chuse the least': Chaucer has it, *c.* 1374, with 'harms' for 'evils'; the latter occurs in *c.* 1440; occasionally the more sensible 'lesser' is used.

Miss. Because Folks would say, when they saw us together; there goes the Woman and her Husband.

'there goes the Woman . . .': Miss clearly wants her husband to be no mere appendage.

Col. [*To Lady* Smart.] Will your Ladyship be on the *Mall* To-morrow Night?

Lady Sm. No, that won't be proper; you know To-morrow is *Sunday.*

Lord Sp. What then, Madam, they say, the better Day the better Deed.

'the better Day the better Deed': the better form (recorded in 1612) of 'the better the day, the better the deed'. Applied especially to Sundays.

Lady Ans. Pray, Mr. *Neverout,* how do you like my Lady *Fruzz?*

Nev. Pox on her, she's as old as *Pole's.*

'Pox on her': usually 'a Pox . . .', as in Shakespeare. – *Pole's* = St Paul's.

Miss. So will you be, if you ben't hang'd when you're young.

Nev. Come, Miss, let us be Friends; will you go to the Park this Evening?

Miss. With all my Heart, and a Piece of my Liver; but not with you.

'with all my Heart, and . . . Liver': this emphatic, perhaps originally humorous, version of 'with all my heart' occurs at least as early as 1598 (Apperson).

Lady Sm. I'll tell you one Thing, and that's not two: I'm afraid I shall get a Fit of the Head-ach To-day.

'I'll tell you one Thing . . .': a catch-phrase that has endured.

Col. O, Madam, don't be afraid, it comes with a Fright.

Miss. [*To Lady* Answerall.] Madam, one of your Ladyship's Lappets is longer than t'other.

'Lappets': probably, streamers of her headdress.

Lady Ans. Well, no Matter; they that ride on a trotting Horse will ne'er perceive it.

'They that ride . . .': apparently a catch-phrase of the period.

Nev. Indeed, Miss, your Lappets hang worse.

Miss. Well, I love a Lyar in my Heart, and you fit me to a Hair.

'I love a Lyar in my Heart': Secretly I admire a liar. Compare the 20th century 'I'm a bit of a liar myself'.

'fit to a Hair': very exactly – hence, very well – indeed.

[*Miss rises up.*]

Nev. Duce take you, Miss, you trod on my Foot, I hope you don't intend to come to my Bed-Side.

Miss. In troth, you are afraid of your Friends, and none of them near you.

> 'afraid of your Friends, and none . . .': in 1699, this is mentioned as 'the old proverb'; obsolete, I think.

Lord Sp. Well said, Girl, [*giving her a Chuck.*] take that, they say a Chuck under the Chin is worth two Kisses.

> 'a Chuck under the Chin . . .': recorded only here?

Lady Answ. But, Mr. *Neverout*, I wonder why such a handsome strait young Gentleman as you, does not get some rich Widow.

Lord Sp. Strait! ay, strait as my Leg, and that's crooked at Knee.

> 'strait [straight] as my Leg . . .': an ironic catch-phrase, now heard but seldom.

Nev. Faith, Madam, if it rain'd rich Widows, none of them would fall upon me. I'gad I was born under a three Penny Planet, never to be worth a Groat.

> 'if it rain'd rich Widows . . .': Neverout's witty modification of the mid-17th–20th century 'If it should rain porridge, he would want' – be without – 'his dish'.
> 'born under a three Penny Planet . . .': to be born poor: 17th–20th centuries; in 19th–20th, mostly rural and with a slightly changed sense. Compare 'If you make not much of three pence, you'll ne'er be worth a groat' (Ray, 1678). *Groats* – coins worth fourpence – had, in 1662, ceased to be coined.

Lady Answ. No, Mr. *Neverout*, I believe you were born with a Cawl on your Head; you are such a Favourite among the Ladies. But, what think you of Widow *Prim?* She's immensely rich.

> 'born with a Cawl on your Head': a caul, or inner membrane enclosing a child before birth and sometimes enclosing its head at birth, was formerly regarded as a good omen; and 'born with a caul' was, until *c.* 1850, synonymous with 'born lucky'.

Nev. Hang her, they say her Father was a Baker.

Lady Sm. Ay, but it is not what is she, but what has she now a-days.

> 'not what is she, but what has she': a handsome *dot* goes a long way. Better still: Don't marry for money, but where the money *is*.

Col. Tom, Faith put on a bold Face for once, and have at the Widow. I'll speak a good Word for you to her.

Lady Ans. Ay, I warrant you'll speak one Word for him, and two for yourself.

Miss. Well, I had that just at my Tongue's End.

'had that just at my Tongue's end' : or, as we say nowadays, 'had it on the tip of my tongue'.

Lady Answ. Why, Miss, they say good Wits jump.

'Good Wits jump' : 17th–19th century, occasionally with 'great' for 'good'. The late 19th–20th century equivalent : 'Great minds think alike'.

Nev. Faith, Madam, I had rather marry a Woman I loved, in her Smock, than Widow *Prim,* if she had her Weight in Gold.

'had her Weight in Gold' : were worth her weight in gold.

Lady Sm. Come, Mr. *Neverout,* Marriage is honourable; but, Housekeeping is a Shrew.

'Marriage is honourable . . .' : 17th–19th centuries. Apparently first thus in Ray, 1670, although adumbrated elsewhere.

Lady Answ. Consider, Mr. *Neverout,* four bare Legs in a Bed; and you are a younger Brother.

'four bare Legs in a Bed' : allusion to the 16th–20th century proverb, 'More belongs' – or 'goes' – 'to marriage than four . . .'

Col. Well, Madam, the younger Brother is the better Gentleman. However, *Tom,* I would advise you to look before you leap.

'the younger Brother . . .' : 17th–19th century. Because his father has longer been a gentleman when he begets the younger son.
'look before you leap' : in 16th–17th century, often 'ere' for 'before'.

Lord Sp. The Colonel says true : Besides, you can't expect to wive and thrive in the same Year.

'can't expect to wive and thrive in the same Year' : marry and prosper. Recorded *c.* 1410 and probably much older than that; rare in the 19th century.

Miss. [*Shuddering.*] Lord, there's some Body walking over my Grave.

'there's some Body walking over my Grave' : still said when one shivers for no apparent reason.

Col. Pray, Lady *Answerall,* where was you last Wednesday, when I did my self the Honour to wait on you? I think your Ladyship is one of the Tribe of Gad.

'one of the Tribe of Gad' or, as Lady Smart has said, some five pages back, 'a very great Gadder abroad' : 17th–19th centuries. A sermon of 1629 has 'The tribe of Levi must have no mind to' –

desire to imitate – 'the tribe of Gad'. One of the Biblical puns so common until *c.* 1914.

Lady Answ. Why, Colonel; I was at Church.

Col. Nay, then I will be hang'd, and my Horse too.

'I will be hang'd . . .' : I'll be damned – *if* it's true!

Nev. I believe her Ladyship was at a Church, with a Chimney in it.

'a Church, with a Chimney in it' : at a private house. A catch-phrase still heard occasionally in the 20th century, with 'in it' omitted.

Miss. Lord! my Pettycoat, how it hangs by Jommetry.

'it hangs by Jommetry' : 'geometry' implies 'at an angle' – crooked. The spelling and pronunciation *jommetry* have been satirized by Swift in his Introduction.

Nev. Perhaps, the Fault may be in your Shape.

Miss. [*Looking gravely.*] Come, Mr. *Neverout,* there's no Jest like a true Jest: But, I suppose, you think my Back's broad enough to bear every Thing.

'no Jest like a true Jest' : compare the better-known 17th–20th century proverb, 'There's many a true word spoken in jest' or 'Many a true word is . . .'

'Back's broad enough . . .' : allusive to 'His back is broad enough to bear jests', current since early in the 17th century; now mostly allusive, in some such form as '*My* back's broad!'

Nev. Madam; I humbly beg your Pardon.

Miss. Well, Sir, your Pardon's granted.

'your Pardon's granted' : a conventional civility; now often, although not at a high social level: 'Granted' or even 'Granted, 'I'm sure'.

Nev. Well, all Things have an End, and a Pudden has two, up up on, my my Word. [*Stutters.*]

'all things have an end . . . two' : a mid-16th–mid-19th century proverb, usually 'Everything hath an end, and . . .', probably at first a jocular extension of the still older 'Everything hath an end'. Nowadays often 'All good things must end'.

Miss. What; Mr. *Neverout,* can't you speak without a Spoon?

'can't you speak . . . ?' : can't you speak without assistance? A spoon on the tongue was supposed to stop stuttering.

Lady Sp. [*To Lady* Smart.] Has your Ladyship seen the Dutchess since your Falling-out?

'Falling-out' : a quarrel.

Lady Sm. Never, my Lord, but once at a Visit; and she look'd at me, as the Devil look'd over *Lincoln*.

'she look'd at me . . . *Lincoln*' : malignly; enviously. A 16th–18th century proverb, the reference being to Lincoln's stately cathedral.

Nev. Pray Miss, take a Pinch of my Snuff.

Miss. What; you break my Head, and give me a Plaister; well, with all my Heart; once and not use it.

'break my Head, and give me a Plaister' (plaster) : a 15th–19th century proverbial saying.
'once and not use it' : a variant of the mid-15th–18th century proverbial phrase, 'once and use it not'.

Nev. Well, Miss, if you wanted me and your Victuals, you'd want your two best Friends.

'if you wanted me and . . .' : if you lacked me and your food, you would lack your two best friends. A special-pleading variant of the 17th–18th (? 19th) century proverbial 'If you wanted me and your meat [i.e. food], you would want one good friend' – meaning, your food.

Col. [*To Neverout.*] *Tom*, Miss and you must kiss and be Friends.

'kiss and be Friends' : current in English since the 13th century (? earlier). Now often merely = decide to be friends again ('make it up').

[*Neverout salutes Miss.*]

Miss. Any Thing for a quiet Life. My Nose itch'd, and I knew I should drink Wine, or kiss a Fool.

'Any Thing for a quiet Life' : 17th (probably also 16th)–20th century. Perhaps popularized by Middleton's play of that title, *c.* 1621.
'My Nose itch'd . . . or kiss a Fool' : an allusion to the 18th–19th century proverb, 'If your nose itches, you will kiss' – or 'shake hands with' – 'a fool'. (Apperson.)

Col. Well, *Tom*, if that ben't fair, hang fair.

Nev. I never said a rude Thing to a Lady in my Life.

Miss. Here's a Pin for that Lye. I'm sure Lyars had need of good Memories. Pray, Colonel, was not he very uncivil to me but just now?

'a Pin for that Lye' : probably elliptical for 'I care not a pin for that lie'.
'Lyars had need of good Memories' : in one variation or another,

'Liars should have good memories' has been current since *c*. 1500. Quintilian, *'Vulgo dicitur, mendacem memorem esse oportere'*. (Apperson.)

Lady Answ. Mr. *Neverout*, if Miss will be angry for nothing, take my Council, and bid her turn the Buckle of her Girdle behind her.

'bid her turn the Buckle . . .': a mid-16th–20th century (latterly, rural) saying, the implication being, apparently, this: a person so angry that he will fight should turn the buckle of his belt to the rear so that it won't hurt his belly if he is punched there.

Nev. Come, Lady *Answerall*, I know better Things, Miss and I are good Friends: Don't put Tricks upon Travellers.

'Don't put Tricks upon Travellers': Don't try to make fools of us: 17th–19th centuries. Don't tell us false tales of strange lands and peoples.

Col. Tom, not a Word of the Pudden, I beg you.

'not a Word of the Pudden': an allusion private to Tom and the Colonel? Or a scabrous insinuation common at the period and since lost?

Lady Sm. Ah, Colonel, you'll never be good, nor then neither.

'you'll never be good, nor then neither': you'll never be good, even if you try.

Lord Sp. Which of the Goods d'ye mean? Good for something, or good for nothing.

Miss. I have a Blister on my Tongue; yet I don't remember I told a Lye.

'a Blister on my Tongue': attributed by folklore to the telling of a lie: an allusion to the 16th–19th Century proverb, 'A blister will rise upon one's tongue that tells a lie'.

Lady Ans. I thought you did just now.

Lord Sp. Pray, Madam, what did thought do?

'what did thought do?': a catch-phrase, still current in the form 'You know what thought did!' – sometimes amplified by 'Kissed another man's wife', to quote the polite version.

Lady Answ. Well, for my Life I cannot conceive what your Lordship means.

Lord Sp. Indeed, Madam, I mean no Harm.

Lady Sm. No to be sure, my Lord, you are as innocent as a Devil of two Year old.

'as innocent as a Devil . . .': first recorded in 1678 and obsolete by 1800, this is a conscious variation of 'as innocent as a new-born babe'.

Nev. Madam, they say, ill Doers, are ill Deemers; but I don't apply it to your Ladyship.

'ill Doers, are ill Deemers' : those who do ill, think (or fear) ill : 18th–19th centuries.

[*Miss mending a Hole in her Lace.*]

Miss. Well, you see I'm mending; I hope, I shall be good in Time. Look, Lady *Answerall,* is it not well mended?

'you see I'm mending . . . good in Time' : Miss puns on her physical and moral health.

Lady Ans. Ay, this is something like a Tanzy.

'a Tanzy' : a 17th–18th century variant of *Tansy,* an upright herb with button-like flowers; hence – the sense here – a pudding, or a custard, flavoured with tansy juice.

Lady Sm. Pray Colonel, are you not very much tann'd?

Col. Yes, Madam, but a Cup of Christmas Ale, will soon wash it off.

Lord Sp. Lady *Smart,* does not your Ladyship think Mrs. *Fade,* is mightily altered since her Marriage?

Lady Answ. Why, my Lord, she was handsome in her Time; but, she can't eat her Cake and have her Cake. I hear she's grown a mere Otomy.

'can't eat her Cake . . .' : a conversational variant of the 16th–20th century proverb, 'You cannot eat your cake and have it' – '*On ne peut pas avoir le drap et l'argent*'.

'a mere Otomy' (usually *atomy,* from *anatomy*) : a walking skeleton.

Lady Answ. Poor Creature, the black Ox has set his Foot upon her already.

'the black Ox . . .' : a variant of the 16th–20th century (in 19th–20th, dialectal) proverb, 'The black ox hath (*or* has) trod (*or* trodden) on one's foot' : care – or old age – has made its black mark on one.

Miss. Ay, she has quite lost the Blue on the Plum.

'lost the Blue on the Plum' : lost her bloom.

Lady Sm. And yet, they say he is very fond of her still.

Lady Answ. O Madam! if she would eat Gold, he would give it her.

'if she would eat Gold . . .' : the saying, which occurs in Mrs Centlivre, 1708, has several precious-metal and precious-stone variations.

Nev. [*To Lady* Smart.] Madam, have you heard that Lady *Queasy,* was lately at the Play-House in Cog?

'... *some Cant Words*' : some words much used in current fashionable slang. Of these seven terms – *in cog, rep, pozz, mobb, fizz, bamb'd, hipps* – all have been mentioned in Swift's Introduction (see my notes 44–51 for comments) and six, the exception being *bamb'd,* in the famous essay in *The Tatler* of September 28, 1710. But '*some Cant Words*' omits *plenipo,* recorded both in Swift's Introduction and in *The Tatler.*
'Lady *Queasy*' : fastidious.
'in Cog' : for *incog,* for Italian *incognito* or feminine *incognita.*

Lady Sm. What Lady *Queasy,* of all Women in the World! Do you say it upon Rep?

'upon Rep' : upon *reputation,* upon your word of honour.

Nev. Pozz; I saw her with my own Eyes; she sat among the Mobb in the Gallery, her own ugly Fizz. And she saw me look at her.

'Pozz' : positively.
'the Mobb' : the Mob : the *mobile vulgus* (fickle crowd) : the rabble.
'ugly Fizz' : ugly *Phiz* or face, from *physiognomy.*

Col. Her Ladyship was plaguily bamb'd; I warrant it put her into the Hipps.

'bamb'd : bamboozled.
'the Hipps' : the *hips* or *hyps* : a fit of *hypo*chondria; here, merely mental depression, discouragement.

Nev. I smoakt her huge Nose; and I'gad, she put me in Mind of the Woodcock, that strives to hide his long Bill, and then thinks no Body sees him.

'I'gad' : now usually written *egad* : *i' Gad*'s (= in God's) name.
'the Woodcock ... thinks no Body sees him' : apparently a verbose conversational allusion to the 16th–18th century proverbial phrase, 'as wise as a woodcock' – brainless, stupid, very foolish.

Col. Tom, I advise you to hold your Tongue; for you'll never say so good a Thing again.
Lady Sm. Miss, what are you looking for?
Miss. O! Madam, I have lost the finest Needle.
Lady Answ. Why, seek 'till you find it, and you won't lose your Labour.

* Here the Author, for Variety, runs into some Cant Words.

'seek till you find it, and . . .': apparently recorded first by Ray, 1678, and apparently obsolete by 1900.

Nev. The Loop of my Hat is broke. How shall I mend it? [*He fastens it with a Pin.*] well, hang them, say I, that have no Shift.
Miss. Ay, and hang them that has one too many.
Miss. Well, but I don't like such Jesting.

'hang them . . . that have no Shift': those who lack ingenuity or, as is so common in the 1960s, 'know-how'. The usual 17th–18th century version is 'Hang him that hath' – or 'has' – 'no shifts'. In 1732, 'Gnomologia' Fuller includes, as part of the saying, 'and hang him that has one too many'. Miss's second speech ('Well, but I . . .') would read better if added, perhaps after a dash, to her first.

Nev. Oh Miss! I have heard a sad Story of you.
Miss. I defy you, Mr. *Neverout;* no Body can say, black's my Eye.

'no Body can say, black's my Eye': nobody can justly slander me: a proverbial saying of the 15th–20th centuries. Elliptical for: '. . . black is the white of my eye'.

Nev. I believe you would wish they could.
Miss. Well, but who was your Author? Come, tell Truth for once, and shame the Devil.

'tell Truth . . . Devil': 16th–20th centuries; after *c.* 1800, usually '. . . the truth . . .'

Nev. Come, then Miss; guess who it was that told me; come, put on your considering Cap.

'put on your considering Cap': think carefully: a proverbial phrase of the 17th–20th centuries.

Miss. Well, who was it?
Nev. Why, one that lives within a Mile of an Oak.

'within a Mile of an Oak': not far away: late 16th–mid-19th centuries. In 16th–17th century England, everyone lived near or, at least, fairly near, an oak tree.

Miss. Well; go hang yourself in your own Garter; for I'm sure the Gallows groans for you.

'go hang yourself . . .': mid-16th–18th century, mostly with plural 'garters'.
'the Gallows groans for you': same period.

Nev. Bite! Miss, I was but in Jest.
Miss. Well, but don't let that stick in your Gizzard.

'stick in your Gizzard' : Don't let that embarrass or worry you! Since *c.* 1650.

Col. [*To Lord* Smart.] My Lord, does your Lordship know Mrs. *Talkall?*

Lord Sm. Only by Sight : But, I hear she has a great deal of Wit; and I'gad, as the Saying is, Mettle to the Back-Bone.

'Mettle to the Back-Bone' : usually 'metal or mettle to the back' – compare Shakespeare's 'steel to the very back' (*Titus Andronicus,* IV, iii) – 'plenty of courage or spirit'. Apparently obsolete by *c.* 1850. Ray, 1678, explains it as 'a metaphor taken from knives and swords'. (Apperson; *ODEP*).

Lady Sm. So I hear.

Col. Why; *Dick Lubber,* said to her t'other Day; Madam, you can't cry Bo to a Goose : Yes, but I can said she; and I'gad cry'd Bo full in his Face. We all thought we should break our Hearts with laughing.

'can't cry Bo to a Goose' : rather less common than '. . . say Bo . . .' : since mid-16th century.

'break our Hearts with laughing' = the 19th–20th century 'die of' – or 'with' – 'laughing' or the occasional 20th century 'burst a blood-vessel with laughing'.

Lord Sp. That was cutting with a Vengeance. And, prithee how did the Fool look?

'with a Vengeance' : intensely. This cliché originated as a picturesque metaphor ('with a curse'), degraded as early as 1568 to 'violently' or 'extremely' (*OED*).

Col. Look : I'gad, he look'd for all the World, like an Owl in an Ivy Bush.

'for all the World' : exactly or utterly. Another cliché; in the Middle Ages, a graphic and effective metaphor.

'an Owl in an Ivy Bush' : 16th–20th centuries; in 19th–20th, mostly rural : 'large-eyed and uncouth : like an owl partly concealed in a bushy branch'.

[*Child comes in screaming.*]

Miss. Well, if that Child was mine, I'd whip it 'till the Blood came. Peace you little Vixen; if I were near you, I wou'd not be far from you.

'if I were near you, I wou'd not be . . .' : if near at all, then very near indeed. Probably a catch-phrase of the period.

Lady Sm. Ay, ay, Batchelor's Wives, and Maid's Children, are finely tutor'd.

'Batchelor's Wives, and Maid's Children . . .': strictly, 'bachelors' wives and maids' children . . .' and usually '. . . well taught': 16th–20th centuries.

Lady Answ. Come to me Master, and I'll give you a Sugar-Plum: Why Miss, you forget that ever you was a Child yourself.

[*She gives the Child a Lump of Sugar.*]

I have heard 'em say Boys will long.

'Come to me Master . . . a Sugar-Plum': 'Come to me, boy' – *master* being the formal address – 'and I'll give you a sweet' (a candy) that, originally shaped like a plum, was made of boiled sugar and variously flavoured and coloured; what, until *c.* 1870, was called a *comfit*.

'Boys will long': boys hanker after sweet things.

Col. My Lord, I suppose you know, that Mr. *Buzzard* has married again.

Lady Sm. This is his fourth Wife; then he has been shod round.

'shod round': short for *shod all round,* of a horse shod on all four feet.

Col. Why, you must know, she had a Month's Mind to *Dick Frontless,* and thought to run away with him; but, her Parents forced her to take the old Fellow, for a good Settlement.

'had a Month's mind to': took a passing fancy to.

Lord Sp. So the Man got his Mare again.

'the Man got his Mare again': an allusion to the proverbial 'The man hath his mare again, and all is' – or 'shall be' – 'well': late 16th–mid-19th century.

Lady Sm. I'm told he said a very good Thing to *Dick;* said he, you *think* us old Fellows are Fools. But we old Fellows *know* young Fellows are Fools.

'you *think* us old Fellows . . . we old Fellows *know* . . .': a version of the 16th–20th century 'Young men think old men fools, and old men know young men to be so'. (Apperson.) Compare Henri Estienne's epigram, published in 1594: *'Si jeunesse savait, si vieillesse pouvait'.*

Col. I know nothing of that; but I know, he's devilish Old, and she's very Young.

Lady Answ. Why, they call that a Match of the World's making.

Miss. What, if he had been Young, and she Old?

Nev. Why, Miss, that would have been a Match of the Devil's making: But, when both are Young, that's a Match of God's making.

'a match of the World's making' : a *mariage de convenance*; 'a match of the Devil's making' or a fool's; 'a match of God's making' or one made in heaven.

[*Miss searching her Pocket for a Thimble, brings out a Nutmeg.*]
Nev. O Miss! have a Care; for if you carry a Nutmeg in your Pocket, you'll certainly be married to an old Man.

'if you carry a Nutmeg . . .' : folk-lore. As a proverb, apparently cited only by Swift.

Miss. Well, and if ever I be married, it shall be to an old Man; they always make the best Husbands : And it is better to be an old Man's Darling, than a young Man's Warling.

'it is better to be an old Man's Darling, than a young Man's Warling' or, as the 19th–20th centuries have it, 'a young man's slave'. A *warling* is a despised person; the word was discarded from the proverb before 1800 (*ODEP*).

Nev. Faith, Miss, if you speak, as you think, I'll give you my Mother for a Maid.

'if you speak . . . Maid' : I simply don't believe you. (His mother being no virgin.) 'I'll give you my mother for a maid' was probably a fashionable catch-phrase.

[*Lady* Smart *rings the Bell.*]
[*Footman comes in.*]
Lady Sm. Harkee, you Fellow, run to my Lady *Match;* and desire she will remember to be here at Six to play at *Quadrille*, d'ye hear, if you fall by the Way, don't stay to get up again.

'Harkee' : hark ye!
'if you fall by the Way . . .' : perhaps an allusion to the 17th–18th century proverb, 'He that falls to-day may be up again to-morrow'.

Footman. Madam, I don't know the House.
Lady Sm. Well, that's not for Want of Ignorance, follow your Nose. Go enquire among the Servants.

'follow your Nose' : go straight ahead and don't stop to think. 16th–20th centuries. Adumbrated by 'follow one's face' (14th century).

[*Footman goes out, and leaves the Door open.*]
Lady Sm. Here, come back you Fellow, why did you leave the Door open : Remember, that a good Servant must always come, when he's call'd, do what he's bid, and shut the Door after him.

'a good Servant . . .' : this proverbial triad of instructions is recorded, 1645, by James Howell in his *Letters*. Compare 'A good

servant should never be in the way and never out of the way'
(Charles II) (Apperson and *ODEP*).

[*The Footman goes out again, and falls down Stairs.*]

Lady Answ. Neck, or nothing. Come down, or I'll fetch you down :
Well, but I hope the poor Fellow has not saved the Hangman a
Labour.

'Neck, or nothing' : a pun, as is her 'Come down, or I'll fetch
you down'. Yet she is kindly – 'I hope the poor fellow hasn't
broken his neck'.

Nev. Pray, Madam, smoak Miss yonder biting her Lips, and playing with her Fan.

Miss. Who's that takes my Name in vain?

'Who's that takes my Name in vain?' : a catch-phrase that comes
from The Bible and is still used often enough.

[*She runs up to them, and falls down.*]

Lady Sm. What, more falling? Do you intend the Frolick should go
round?

'Do you intend the Frolick . . .?' : are we all to join in the game
and fall down?

Lady Ans. Why, Miss, I wish you may not have broke her Ladyship's Floor.

'may not have broke her Ladyship's Floor' : perhaps an ostensibly
callous catch-phrase.

Nev. Miss, come to me, and I'll take you up.

Lord Sp. Well, but without a Jest, I hope, Miss, you are not hurt.

Col. Nay, she must be hurt for certain; for you see her Head is all
of a Lump.

'hurt for certain; for . . . her Head . . .' : probably another such
catch-phrase.

Miss. Well; remember this, Colonel, when I have Money, and you
have none.

'when I have Money . . .' : I sha'n't give (or lend) you any.
There'll come a day . . . .

Lady Sm. But, Colonel, when do you design to get a House, and a
Wife, and a Fire to put her in?

'get a House . . . a Fire to put her in?' : J. Kelly, *Scotish Proverbs*,
1721, has the proverb to which Lady Smart alludes : 'Never look
for a wife, till you have a house, and a fire to put her in'; and he
adds : 'The jest is in *a fire to put her in,* a house to put her in, and
a fire to set her by'. (Cited by *ODEP*.)

Miss. Lord! who would be married to a Soldier, and carry his Knap-Sack.

> 'married to a Soldier . . .' : and follow him in his campaigns.

Nev. O, Madam, *Mars* and *Venus,* you know.

> '*Mars* and *Venus*' : an allusion to the traditional mutual attraction of 'fair women and brave men'.

Col. I'gad, Madam, I'd marry To-morrow, if I thought I could bury my Wife just when the Honey Moon is over; but they say, a Woman has as many Lives as a Cat.

> 'the Honey Moon' : the customary *month* of *sweet* vacation immediately subsequent to the wedding, but, as the *OED* so neatly puts it, 'originally . . . comparing the mutual affection of newly married persons to the changing moon which is no sooner full than it begins to wane' – what a slander on any true marriage!
> 'a Woman has as many Lives as a Cat' : allusive to a cat's 'nine lives' and varying the 16th–18th century proverb, 'A woman hath' – or 'has' – 'nine lives like a cat'.

Lady Answ. I find, the Colonel thinks a dead Wife under the Table, is the best Goods in a Man's House.

> 'a dead Wife under the Table . . .' : recorded by Ray in 1678.

Lady Sm. O, but Colonel, if you had a good Wife, it would break your Heart to part with her.

Col. Yes, Madam, for they say, he that has lost his Wife and Sixpence, has lost a Tester.

> 'he that has lost his Wife and sixpence . . .' : a 'tester' *is* a sixpence. Recorded by Ray in 1670 as 'He that loseth his wife and sixpence hath lost a tester'; in the 1678 edition, Ray has the short-lived version, 'He that loses his wife and a farthing, hath a great loss of his farthing' with its Italian original.

Lady Sm. But, Colonel, they say, that every married Man should believe there is but one good Wife in the World, and that's his own.

> 'every married Man should believe . . .' : 17th–19th centuries.

Col. For all that, I doubt, a good Wife must be bespoke; for there is none ready made.

> 'bespoke' : bespoken – commissioned or ordered.

Miss. I suppose, the Gentleman's a Woman Hater; but, Sir, I think you ought to remember that once you had a Mother. And, pray, if it had not been for a Woman, where would you have been, Colonel?

> 'once you had a Mother' : a traditional retort.

Col. Nay, Miss, you cry'd Whore first, when you talk'd of the Knap-Sack.

'you cry'd Whore': mentioned the subject of whores.

Lady Answ. But, I hope, you won't blame the whole Sex, because some are bad.

Nev. And, they say, he that hates Women, suck'd a Sow.

'he that hates Women . . .': was suckled by a sow and sub-consciously and illogically disgusted with women: a mid-17th–18th century proverb.

Col. O, Madam, there's no general Rule without an Exception.

'no general Rule without an Exception': a conversational allusion to 'The exception proves the rule' (tests it): a 17th–20th (? earlier) proverb, deriving from Latin.

Lady Sm. Then, why don't you marry and settle.

Col. I'gad, Madam, there's nothing will settle me but a Bullet.

'nothing will settle me but a Bullet': compare the mid-16th–20th century proverb, 'Every bullet has its billet' and the 1914–1918 British soldiers' catch-phrase, used by wounded men, 'It had my number (or, name) on it'.

Miss. I suppose, the Colonel was cross'd in his first Love; which makes him so severe on all the Sex.

'crossed in . . . Love' – thwarted in love – occurs in Steele, 1711, and probably much earlier. Compare *star-crossed*, ill-fated.

Lady Ans. Yes, and I'll hold an hundred to one, that the Colonel has been over Head and Ears in Love with some Lady that has made his Heart ach.

'over Head and Ears in Love': the base or unit is *over head and ears* – for instance, in love or debt or trouble.

Col. O, Madam, we Soldiers are Admirers of all the fair Sex.

'we Soldiers . . . the fair Sex': compare '*Mars* and *Venus*' above.

Miss. I wish I could see the Colonel in love, 'till he was ready to dye.

Lady Sm. Ay, but I doubt, few People dye for Love in these Days.

'few People dye for Love in these Days' – but then, they never did. Yet there is such a malady as love-sickness, and, although very rare, such a death.

Nev. Well, I confess, I differ from the Colonel, for I hope to have a rich, and a handsome Wife yet, before I dye.

Col. Ay, *Tom*, live Horse, and thou shalt have Grass.

'live Horse, and thou shalt have Grass' : live, horse, and . . ., the secret being to keep on keeping on. Apparently a proverb, recorded only (?) in Swift.

Miss. Well, Colonel, but whatever you say against Women, they are better Creatures than Men; for Men were made of Clay, but Woman was made of Man.

'Men were made of Clay, but . . .' : semi-proverbial : semi-allusive to the Biblical story.

Col. Miss, you may say what you please; but faith, you'll never lead Apes in Hell.

'lead Apes in Hell' : be an old maid : mid-16th–19th centuries. Already in 1605 (*ODEP*) mentioned as 'an old proverb'.

Nev. No, no, I'll be sworn, Miss has not an Inch of Nun's Flesh about her.

'not an Inch of Nun's Flesh' : not the material that produces old maids.

Miss. I understumble you, Gentlemen.

'understumble' : a mid-16th–20th century pun on *understand*. Compare the dialectal *undercumstand* and the mid-19th–20th century slang *undercumstumble*.

Nev. Madam, your humblecumdumble.

'your humblecumdumble' : your humble servant. A rhyming reduplication of *humble;* forming with *understumble* a sort of internal crambo.

Lord Sp. Pray, Miss, when did you see your old Acquaintance Mrs. *Cloudy?* You and she are two, I hear.

'You and she are two' : not one; hence, at odds, not friends.

Miss. See her : Marry I don't Care whether I ever see her again, God bless my Eye-Sight.

'God bless my Eye-sight' : and my sight is good, thank Heaven !

Lady Ans. Lord; why she and you were as great as two Inkle-Weavers. I am sure, I have seen her hug you, as the Devil hugg'd the Witch.

'as great as two Inkle-Weavers' : intimate : often 'as thick . . .' (late 17th–20th centuries, latterly rural and, even in dialect, rare by 1940). *Inkle-weavers* (or *makers*)=weavers of linen tape; they worked very close – and closely – together.
'as the Devil hugg'd the Witch' (hard or close) : usually 'as the Devil hugs a Witch' : mid-17th–19th century.

Miss. That's true; but I'm told for certain, she's no better than she should be.

'she's no better than she should be' : a loose, free-loving woman ('Elle ne vaut pas grand chose') : 17th–20th centuries. One of the most famous of all euphemisms.

Lady Sm. Well; God mend us all; but you must allow, the World is very censorious. I never heard that she was naughty.

'naughty' : sexually lax.

Col. [*To* Neverout.] Come, Sir *Thomas,* when the King pleases, when do you intend to march?

'Come, Sir Thomas' : ironic for 'Well, Tom, when do you intend to leave?'

Lord Sp. Have Patience; *Tom,* is your Friend *Ned Rattle* marryed?
Nev. Yes, Faith, my Lord; he has tyed a Knot with his Tongue, that he can never untye with his Teeth.

'tyed a Knot with his Tongue . . . Teeth' : with slight variations, current throughout the approximate period 1550–1850.

Lady Sm. Ay, marry in haste, and repent at leisure.

'marry in haste . . .' : common since the mid-16th century and having Classical forebears.

Lady Answ. Has he got a good Fortune with his Lady? For, they say, something has some savour, but nothing has no flavour.

'something has some savour . . .' : a rhyming 18th–19th century elaboration of the 16th–17th 'Somewhat' – or 'Something' – 'hath (or, will have) some savour'.

Nev. Faith, Madam, all he gets by her, he may put into his Eye, and see never the worse.

'he may put into his Eye . . .' : 16th–20th centuries, often with 'none' for 'never'. Precisely nothing.

Miss. Then, I believe, he heartily wishes her in *Abraham's* Bosom.

'wishes her in *Abraham's* Bosom' : dead. Based on Luke, xvi, 23, 'He seeth Abraham afar off, and Lazarus in his bosom'; Shakespeare established the phrase in English.

Col. Pray, my Lord, how does *Charles Limber,* and his fine Wife agree?
Lord Sp. Why, they say, he's the greatest Cuckold in Town.
Nev. O but, my Lord, you should always except my Lord Mayor.

'you should always except my Lord Mayor' : an allusion to the mid-17th–18th century proverbial advice, 'Good manners to except . . .' – which implies that too sweeping a statement has been made.

Miss. Mr. *Neverout.*

Nev. Hay, Madam, did you call me?

Miss. Hay! Why; Hay is for Horses.

> '*Nev.* Hay, Madam, did you call me? – *Miss.* Hay! Why; Hay is for Horses' : the prototype of '*A* is for 'orses' in the comic phonetic alphabet. See especially my *Comic Alphabets*, 1961.

Nev. Why, Miss, than you may——

Col. Pray, my Lord, what's a Clock by your Oracle?

> 'what's a Clock by your Oracle?' : what time (*o'clock*) is it by your watch? A watch, 'infallibly' telling the correct time, is in its own way an oracle. Slang *oracle* contains perhaps a pun on Latin and Spanish *hora,* Italian *ora,* hour.

Lord Sp. Faith, I can't tell; I think my Watch runs upon Wheels.

> 'my Watch runs upon Wheels' : as, of course, it does. A catch-phrase of the period.

Nev. Miss, pray be so kind to call a Servant to bring me a Glass of Small-Beer. I know you are at Home here.

Miss. Every Fool can do as they're bid. Make a Page of your own Age, and do it yourself.

> 'Make a Page . . . do it yourself' : tautologous, for 'make a page of your own age' = do it yourself. 17th–mid 18th centuries.

Nev. Chuse proud Fool; I did but ask you.

[Miss puts her Hand to her Knee.]

What, Miss, are you thinking of your Sweetheart? Is your Garter slipping down?

> 'Chuse proud Fool; I did but ask you' : Don't be so proud – I merely asked.
>
> 'are you thinking of your Sweetheart? Is . . .?' Like the preceding sentence, this one sounds as if it might contain a catch-phrase. But I cannot prove that it does.

Miss. Pray, Mr. *Neverout,* keep your Breath to cool your Porridge. You measure my Corn by your Bushel.

> 'keep your Breath . . .' : with variants 'save' for 'keep' and 'pottage' (early), this saying goes back to the 16th century.
>
> 'You measure my Corn . . .' : 17th–20th century; since *c.* 1850, mostly rural.

Nev. Indeed, Miss, you Lye——

Miss. Did you ever hear any Thing so rude.

Nev. I mean, you lye——under a Mistake.

'you lye – under a Mistake' (are wrong) : one of (one supposes) hundreds of puns on *lie,* to tell an untruth, and *lie,* to be recumbent.

Miss. If a thousand Lyes could choak you, you would have been choaked many a Day ago.

'If a thousand Lyes . . .' : compare Ray, 1678, 'If a lie could have choked him, that would have done it'. Extant – in one form or another.

[*Miss tries to snatch Mr.* Neverout's *Snuff-Box.*]

Nev. Madam, you miss'd that, as you miss'd your Mother's Blessing.

'as you miss'd your Mother's Blessing' : apparently a catch-phrase.

[*She tries again, and misses.*]

Nev. Snap short makes you look so lean, Miss.

'snap short makes you look so lean' : also 'snapping so short . . .' (Ray, 1678), the reference being to a reach too short.

Miss. Poh; you are so robustious : You had like to put out my Eye : I assure you, if you blind me, you must lead me.

'Poh' : pooh !
'if you blind me . . .' : one feels that Miss would like nothing better than – at least – to be led. (Not, I think, a proverbial saying : possibly a catch-phrase.)

Lady Sm. Dear Miss, be quiet; and bring me a Pin-Cushion out of that Closet.

[*Miss opens the Door, and squals.*]

Lady Sm. Lord bless the Girl, what's the Matter now?

Miss. I vow, Madam, I saw something in black, I thought it was a Spirit.

Col. Why, Miss, did you ever see a Spirit?

Miss. No, Sir, I thank God, I never saw any Thing worse than my self.

'Why, Miss, did you ever see a Spirit? – *Miss.* No, . . . I never saw anything . . .' : fishing for compliments?

Nev. Well, I did a very foolish Thing Yesterday, and was a great Puppy for my Pains.

Miss. Very likely; for they say, many a true Word spoken in Jest.

'many a true Word spoken in Jest' : 17th–20th centuries, adumbrated by Chaucer; already quoted by Swift in this very dialogue.

[*Footman returns.*]

Lady Sm. Well, did you deliver your Message? You are fit to be sent for Sorrow, you stay so long by the Way.

'fit to be sent for Sorrow . . .': contrast 16th–18th (? 19th) century proverb, 'God send you joy, for sorrow will come fast enough'. A bearer of bad tidings is loath to arrive.

Footman. Madam, my Lady was not at home; so, I did not leave the Message.

Lady Sm. This it is to send a Fool of an Errand.

'This it is to send a Fool of an Errand' ('of' = on): apparently an allusion to the 17th–18th century proverb, 'He that sends a fool means to follow him'.

[*Lord* Sparkish *looking at his Watch.*]

Lord Sp. 'Tis past twelve a Clock.

Lady Sm. Well, what is that among us all?

'Well, what is that among us all?': Well, what of it? We're all friends here.

Lord Sp. Madam, I must take my Leave.

Lady Sm. Well, but your Lordship, and the Colonel, will dine with us To-Day; and Mr. *Neverout,* I hope, we shall have your good Company. There will be no Soul else, besides my own Lord, and these Ladies. For every Body knows, I hate a Crowd: I would rather want Vittels, than Elbow Room. We dine punctually at three.

'I would rather want Vittels than Elbow Room.' The phonetic spelling *vittels* was common in the 16th–18th centuries, nor unknown later.

'dine punctually at three': the big meal of the day, and often lasting for two or three hours.

Lord Sp. Madam, we'll be sure to attend your Ladyship.

Col. Madam, my Stomach serves me instead of a Clock.

'my Stomach serves me instead of a Clock': compare the 17th–20th century (latterly rural) saying, 'My belly cries cupboard' – which occurs in the next Conversation.

[*Another Footman comes back.*]

Lady Sm. O, you are the other Fellow I sent: Well, have you been with my Lady *Club.* You are good to send of a dead Man's Errand.

'You are good to send of a dead Man's Errand': Ray, 1670, has 'bodies' for 'man's'. Compare 'fit to be sent for Sorrow' above.

Footman. Madam, my Lady *Club* begs your Ladyship's Pardon; but she is engaged To-Night.

Miss. Well, Mr. *Neverout;* here's the Back of my Hand to you.

'here's the Back of my Hand to you': a flippant (and challenging?) goodbye.

Nev. Miss, I find you will have the last Word. Ladies, I am more yours than my own.

'more yours than my own': a conventional courtesy – I am entirely at your service; or perhaps, as he looks at Miss, I leave my heart with you.

Second Conversation

[*Lord* Smart, *and the former Company at three a Clock, coming to dine.*]

[*After Salutations.*]

Lord Sm. I'M sorry I was not at home this Morning, when you all did us the Honour to call here. But I went to the Levee To-Day.

Lord Sp. O, my Lord; I'm sure the Loss was ours.

> 'the Loss was ours' : a courteous catch-phrase, perhaps a witty convention, that has survived. The tense of the verb naturally varies.

Lady Sm. Gentlemen, and Ladies, you are come into a sad dirty House, I am sorry for it, but we have had our Hands in Mortar.

> 'have had our Hands in Mortar' : either 'We've had the builders in' or, less probably here, 'We've been messing about, trying to do our own repairs'. Compare the 17th–18th century phrase, 'to dip (*or* have *or* put) one's finger in mortar' – to dabble in building.

Lord Sp. O, Madam, your Ladyship is pleased to say so, but I never saw any Thing so clean and so fine. I profess it is a perfect Paradise.

> 'a perfect Paradise' : has become a cliché.

Lady Sm. My Lord, your Lordship is always very obliging.

Lord Sp. Pray, Madam, whose Picture is that?

Lady Sm. Why, my Lord, it was drawn for me.

Lord Sp. I'll swear, the Painter did not flatter your Ladyship.

> 'the Painter did not flatter your Ladyship' : a conventional compliment.

Col. My Lord, the Day is finely cleared up.

Lord Sm. Ay, Colonel, 'tis a Pity that fair Weather should ever do any harm. [*to* Neverout.] Why, *Tom,* you are high in the Mode.

> 'high in the Mode' : very fashionably dressed.

Nev. My Lord, it is better to be out of the World, than out of the Fashion.

> 'it is better to be out of the World . . .' : either thus or 'as good . . ., as out . . .', this very common 17th–18th century proverb has survived.

Lord Sm. But, *Tom,* I hear, you and Miss are always quarelling : I fear, it is your Fault, for I can assure you, she is very good humoured.

Nev. Ay, my Lord, so is the Devil when he's pleas'd.

'very good humoured. – *Nev.* Ay, . . . so is the Devil when he's pleas'd' : usually 'the devil is good' – or 'a good fellow' – 'when he is pleased' : mid-16th–mid-19th centuries.

Lord Sm. Miss, what do you think of my Friend *Tom?*

Miss. My Lord, I think he is not the wisest Man in the World; and truly, he's sometimes very rude.

Lord Sp. That may be true; but yet, he that hangs *Tom* for a Fool, may find a Knave in the Halter.

'he that hangs *Tom* for a Fool, may find a Knave in the Halter' : more knave than fool; intelligent rather than stupid. A left-handed compliment of the 17th–18th centuries. Compare 'more knave than fool' – which comes later in this dialogue.

Miss. Well, however, I wish he were hang'd, if it were only to try.

'if it were only to try' : if only for the sake of the experiment.

Nev. Well, Miss, if I must be hanged, I won't go far to chuse my Gallows : It shall be about your fair Neck.

'hanged . . . about your fair Neck' : evidently a consummation he desires.

Miss. I'll see your Nose Cheese first, and the Dogs eating it. But, my *Lord,* Mr. *Neverout's* Wit begins to run low, for I vow he said this before. Pray, Colonel, give him a Pinch, and I'll do as much for you.

'I'll see your Nose Cheese first . . .' : J. Kelly, *Scotish Proverbs,* 1721, has 'I would sooner see your nose cheese, and my self the first bite' and comments thus, 'a disdainful rejecting of an unworthy proposal'.

'give him a Pinch' : either to see whether he's awake or, more aptly, in allusion to the very old children's round game 'Pinch me'.

Lord Sp. My Lady *Smart,* your Ladyship has a very fine Scarf.

Lady Sm. Yes, my Lord, it will make a flaming Figure in a Country Church.

'make a flaming Figure in a Country Church' : Ray, 1670, has '. . . a fair show . . .' (a pretty sight) : apparently a mid-17th–mid 18th century irony.

[Footman comes in.]

Footman. Madam, Dinner's upon the Table.

Col. Faith, I'm glad of it; my Belly began to cry Cupboard.

'my Belly began to cry Cupboard' : usually '(one's) belly cries cupboard' : mid-17th–20th centuries; in 19th–20th mainly rural.

Nev. I wish I may never hear worse News.

'I wish I may never hear worse News' : partly a conventional
courtesy and partly a catch-phrase; not quite obsolete.

Miss. What; Mr. *Neverout,* you are in great haste; I believe your
Belly thinks your Throat's cut.

'your Belly thinks your Throat's cut' : this still current saying goes
back to early in the 16th century. Compare, above, 'my Belly
began . . .'

Nev. No, faith Miss, three Meals a Day, and a good Supper at night,
will serve my Turn.

'three Meals a Day, and . . .' : I merely want enough, providing
there's plenty.

Miss. To say the Truth, I'm hungry.

Nev. And I'm angry, so let us both go fight.

[*They go in to Dinner, and after the usual Compliments, take their
Seats.*]

Lord Sm. Ladies and Gentlemen, will you eat any Oysters before
Dinner.

Col. With all my Heart. [*Takes an Oyster.*] He was a bold Man that
first eat an Oyster.

'He was a bold Man . . .' : mid-17th–mid 19th century proverb.
Compare : 'Oysters are a cruel meat . . .'.

Lady Sm. They say, Oysters are a cruel Meat; because we eat them
alive : Then, they are an uncharitable Meat; for we leave nothing to
the Poor. And, they are an ungodly Meat, because we never say
Grace to them.

'Oysters are a cruel Meat . . . never say Grace to them' : in this
particular form, first recorded here; another form – 'Oysters are
ungodly . . .' – goes back to the beginning of the 17th century or
perhaps earlier.

Nev. Faith, that's as well said, as if I had said it my self.

'that's as well said, as if . . .' : either a catch-phrase that has endured or, more probably, a Swiftian felicity that has become a
famous quotation.

Lady Sm. Well, we are all well set, if we be but as well serv'd. Come,
Colonel, handle your Arms : Shall I help you to some Beef ?

'Come, Colonel, handle your Arms' : an allusion to his profession,
knife being likened to sword.

Col. If your Ladyship pleases; and pray don't cut like a Mother-in-law, but send me a large Slice; for I love to lay a good Foundation : I vow 'tis a noble Sirloyn.

> 'pray don't cut like a Mother-in-law' : compare the New Forest proverb, 'There is but one good mother-in-law, and she is dead'. As untrue as it is trenchant.
>
> 'lay a good Foundation' : to enable one to face the day's remainder. A metaphor from building : body-building.

Nev. Ay, here's Cut and come again.

Miss. But pray, why is it called a Sirloyn?

Lord Sp. Why, you must know, that our King *James* I. who loved good Eating, being invited to Dinner by one of his Nobles, and seeing a large Loyn of Beef at his Table; he drew out his Sword, and in a Frolick Knighted it. Few People know the Secret of this.

> 'why is it called a Sirloyn? *Lord Sp.* [? rather *Lord Sm.*] . . . Few People know the Secret of this' : and this is not the secret, but merely one of several such anecdotes. Ernest Weekley succinctly derives it thus : 'Earlier *surloyn, OF. surloigne,* over-loin'; simply the upper (and choicer) part of a loin of beef.

Lady Sm. Beef is Man's Meat, my Lord.

Lord Sm. But, my Lord, I say, Beef is the King of Meat.

Miss. Pray, what have I done, that I must not have a Plate?

Lady Sm. [*To* Lady *Answerall.*] What will your Ladyship please to eat?

Lady Answ. Pray, Madam, help your self.

Col. They say Eating and Scratching wants but a Beginning. If you will give me Leave, I'll help my self to a Slice of this Shoulder of Veal.

> 'Eating and Scratching wants but a Beginning' : once you start, it's hard to stop. I suspect that this proverb is merely a variant of 'Eating and drinking wants but a beginning', likewise recorded by Kelly in 1721. Compare Rabelais's 'L'appétit vient en mangeant'.

Lady Sm. Colonel, you can't do a kinder Thing. Well, you are all heartily welcome, as I may say.

> 'You are all heartily welcome' : interesting and revealing, the extent to which these old courtesies have survived! Compare the mid-17th–mid-19th century invitation to a friend : 'Eat, and welcome; eat fast [=well], and heartily welcome'.

Col. They say there are thirty and two good Bits in a Shoulder of Veal.

'thirty and two good bits in a Shoulder of Veal' : Ray, 1678, has
'In a shoulder of veal there are twenty and two good bits' and
adds that 'This is a piece of country wit. They mean by it, There
are twenty (others say forty) bits in a shoulder of veal, and but two
good ones'. Lady Smart's 'thirty bad Bits, and two good ones' pro-
vides the right comment.

Lady Sm. Ay, Colonel; thirty bad Bits, and two good ones; you see
I understand you; but, I hope you have got one of the two good
ones?
Nev. Colonel, I'll be of your Mess.

'Colonel, I'll be of your Mess' : I'll copy you. Tom continues the
game of addressing the colonel in military terms.

Col. Then, pray *Tom,* carve for your self : They say, two Hands in
a Dish, and one in a Purse. Hah, said I well, *Tom?*

'two Hands in a Dish, and one in a Purse' : a 17th–mid-19th century proverb. The two hands, one's own; that in a purse, one's
own.

Nev. Colonel, you spoke like an Oracle.

'you spoke like an Oracle' : now, accurately and authoritatively;
but originally, darkly and deviously.

[*Miss to Lady* Answerall.]
Miss. Madam, will your Ladyship help me to some Fish?
Lord Sm. [*To* Neverout.] *Tom,* they say Fish should swim thrice.
Nev. How is that, my Lord?
Lord Sm. Why, *Tom,* first it should swim in the Sea; (do you mind
me?) then it should swim in Butter; and at last Sirrah, it should swim
in good Claret. I think I have made it out.

'Fish should swim thrice. – *Nev.* How is that . . .? – *Lord Sm.*
Why, Tom, first . . . then . . . at last . . .' : in Cotgrave's dictionary,
1611, it is twice (water and wine); in Ray, 1670, very much as in
Swift.
'have made it out' : have got it right.

[*Footman to Lord* Smart.]
Footman. My Lord, Sir *John Linger* is coming up.
Lord Sm. God so ! I invited him to Dinner with me to-Day, and
forgot it. Well, desire him to walk in.

'God so!' : Good heavens ! He would be, of course. Strictly, *Godso*
is a variant of *Gadso,* itself a euphemism for *catso.*

[*Sir* John Linger *comes in.*]

Sir John. What, are you at it? Why, then I'll be gone.

Lady Sm. Sir *John,* I beg you will set down; come, the more, the merrier.

Sir John. Ay; but the fewer the better Cheer.

> 'the more, the merrier . . . but the fewer the better Cheer': the full form (16th–18th centuries) of *the more, the merrier* (16th–20th centuries); *fare* commoner than *cheer.*

Lady Sm. Well, I am the worst in the World at making Apologies. It was my Lord's Fault. I doubt you must kiss the Hare's Foot.

> 'you must kiss the Hare's Foot': to 'dine with Duke Humphrey' or go without or be too late: late 16th–mid-19th centuries. Variant: 'lick' for 'kiss'.

Sir John. I see you are fast by the Teeth.

> 'fast by the Teeth': with one's teeth firmly engaged and embedded.

Col. Faith, Sir *John,* we are killing that would kill us.

> 'killing that would kill us': eating what would kill us. A reference to beef. Hence 'a business of Life and Death' or, logically, life or death.

Lord Sp. You see, Sir *John,* we are upon a Business of Life and Death. Come, will you do as we do. You are come in Pudden Time.

> 'in Pudden time': not in time for pudding, as one might suppose, but at the right moment: a proverbial phrase of the 16th–19th centuries.

Sir John. Ay, this you would be doing if I were dead. What, you keep Court Hours I see. I'll be going, and get a Bit of Meat at my Inn.

> 'this you would be doing if I were dead': . . . even though I were (recently) dead.

Lady Sm. Why, we won't eat you, Sir *John.*

> 'we won't eat you': we're not dangerous. A catch-phrase; extant.

Sir John. It is my own Fault; but, I was kept by a Fellow, who bought some *Derbyshire* Oxen from me.

> '*Derbyshire* Oxen': cattle-farming in the Derbyshire dales has long been famed.

Nev. You see, Sir *John,* we stayed for you, as one Horse does for another.

> 'stayed . . . as one Horse does for another': probably, as the *ODEP* holds, a proverbial saying.

Lady Sm. My Lord, will you help Sir *John* to some Beef. Lady *Answerall,* pray eat, you see your Dinner. I am sure, if we had known we should have such good Company, we should have been better provided; but, you must take the Will for the Deed. I'm afraid you are invited to your Loss.

> 'take the Will for the Deed' : proverbial phrase, common since the 15th century.

Col. And, pray, Sir *John,* how do you like the Town? You have been absent a long Time.

Sir John. Why, I find little *London* stands just where it did when I left it last.

> 'I find little *London* stands just where it did.' At least he doesn't call it 'little old London'! Compare the famous 'Stands Scotland where it did?' – a quotation (Shakespeare, *Macbeth,* IV, iii, 164) that has become a jocular catch-phrase.

Nev. What do you think of *Hanover-Square,* why, Sir *John, London* is gone out of Town since you saw it.

> '*London* is gone out of Town' : grown tremendously since you saw it last. Hanover Square was begun *c.* 1715.

Lady Sm. Sir *John,* I can only say, you are heartily welcome; and I wish I had something better for you.

Col. Here's no Salt; Cuckolds will run away with the Meat.

> 'here's no Salt; Cuckolds . . .' : Ray, 1678, explains the proverb, 'If a cuckold come he'll take away the meat', thus : 'viz. If there be no salt on the table'.

Lord Sm. Pray edge a little to make more Room for Sir *John.* Sir *John* fall to, you know half an Hour is soon lost at Dinner.

> 'Pray edge a little' : move, or re-arrange yourselves, a little.
> 'half an Hour is soon lost at Dinner' : a jocularly ironic catch-phrase (recorded only in Swift) – reminiscent of very long sessions.

Sir John. I protest, I can't eat a Bit; for I took Share of a Beef-Stake, and two Mugs of Ale with my Chapman, besides a Tankard of *March* Beer as soon as I got out of Bed.

> 'Beef-Stake' : beef steak; recorded in 1711, but probably a decade older.
> 'my Chapman' : usually 'dealer'; here, probably 'agent'.
> '*March* beer' : strong, and brewed in March.

Lady Answ. Not fresh and fasting, I hope.

> 'fresh and fasting'; without eating some food beforehand.

Sir John. Yes faith, Madam, I always wash my Kettle before I put the Meat in it.

> 'wash my Kettle . . .': put liquor into my stomach.

Lady Sm. Poh! Sir *John,* you have seen nine Houses since you eat last: Come, you have kept a Corner of your Stomach for a Bit of Venison-Pasty.

> 'a Corner . . . for a Bit of Venison-Pasty': 'Which Dr Goldsmith remembered in immortal verse' (Saintsbury).

Sir John. Well, I'll try what I can do when it comes up.

Lady Answ. Come, Sir *John,* you may go further, and fare worse.

> 'go further, and fare worse': 16th–20th centuries; variants, 'farther' and 'far'.

Miss. [*To* Neverout.] Pray, Mr. *Neverout,* will you please to send me a Piece of Tongue?

Nev. By no Means, Madam; one Tongue's enough for a Woman.

> 'one Tongue's enough . . .': recorded by Ray, 1678; obsolete by 1900.

Col. Miss, here's a Tongue that never told a Lye.

> 'a Tongue that never told a Lye': a tongue cooked for food.

Miss. That was because it could not speak. Why, Colonel, I never told a Lye in my Life.

Nev. I appeal to all the Company, whether that be not the greatest Lye that ever was told.

Col. [*To* Neverout.] Prethee, *Tom,* send me the two Legs, and Rump, and Liver, of that Pigeon; for you must know, I love what no Body else loves.

> 'Prethee': I pray thee, I ask you: *prethee,* for the much commoner *prithee,* is a mainly 17th century form, the Colonel's speech being very slightly old-fashioned.

Nev. But what if any of the Ladies should long. Well, here take it, and the Devil do you good with it.

> 'the Devil do you good with it': I hope you enjoy it.

Lady Answ. Well; this eating and drinking takes away a Body's Stomach.

> 'eating and drinking takes away . . .': 17th–20th centuries; rare since *c.* 1920. Here, stomach = appetite.

Nev. I'm sure I have lost mine.

Miss. What! the Bottom of it, I suppose.

'I'm sure I've lost mine. – What, the Bottom of it, I suppose' : im-
plying a bottomless belly or an insatiable appetite.

Nev. No really, Miss, I have quite lost it.

Miss. I should be sorry a poor Body had found it.

Lady Sm. But, Sir *John,* we hear you are marryed since we saw
you last. What; you have stolen a Wedding, it seems.

'stolen a Wedding' : accomplished secretly or unnoticed – and thus
deprived us of – a wedding.

Sir John. Well, one can't do a foolish Thing once in one's Life, but
one must hear of it a hundred Times.

'one can't do a foolish Thing . . .' : well, well, that's human nature
for you!

Col. And pray, Sir *John,* how does your Lady unknown?

Sir John. My Wife's well, Colonel; and at your Service in a civil
Way. Ha, ha. [*He laughs.*]

'at your Service in a civil Way. Ha, ha' : never opens his mouth
without putting his foot in it.

Miss. Pray, Sir *John,* is your Lady tall, or short?

Sir John. Why, Miss, I thank God, she's a little Evil.

'she's a little Evil' : she is a little woman and therefore a minor
evil – in allusion to the old masculine proverb, 'Women are
necessary evils'.

Lord Sp. Come, give me a Glass of Claret.

[*Footman fills him a Bumper.*]

Why do you fill so much?

Nev. My Lord, he fills as he loves you.

Lady Sm. Miss, shall I send you some Cucumber?

Miss. Madam, I dare not touch it; for they say, Cucumbers are cold
in the third Degree.

'Cucumbers are cold in the third Degree' : perhaps compare the
simile, 'as cool as a cucumber', and certainly compare Fletcher's
'Young maids were as cold as cucumbers' (*Cupid's Revenge,* I, i).
Apperson.

Lady Sm. Mr. *Neverout,* do you love Pudden?

Nev. Madam, I'm like all Fools; I love every Thing that is good :
But the Proof of the Pudden, is in the eating.

'I'm like all Fools; I love . . .' : has occurred in the first Dialogue.
'the Proof of the Pudden . . .' : 17th–20th centuries. The spelling
pudden goes back to the 16th century and, when not dialectal, it
was colloquial until *c.* 1800 and then illiterate.

Col. Sir *John,* I hear you are a great Walker, when you are at home.
Sir John. No, Faith, Colonel, I always love to walk with a Horse in my Hand. But I have had devilish bad Luck in Horse-Flesh, of late.
Lady Sm. Why then, Sir *John,* you must kiss a Parson's Wife.

> 'love to walk with a Horse in my hand' : to go on horseback, to ride. Probably in allusion to the mid 16th–18th century proverb, 'It is good walking with a horse in one's hand' – explained by Kelly, 1721, thus : 'It is good when a man of any art, trade, or profession, has an estate to support him, if these should fail' (Apperson; *ODEP*).
> 'devilish bad Luck in Horse-Flesh ... Why then, ... you must kiss a Parson's Wife' : the 17th–mid-19th century proverb runs, 'He that would have good luck in horses, must kiss the parson's wife'. Based on folklore?

Lady Sm. They say, Sir *John,* that your Lady has a great deal of Wit.
Sir John. Madam, she can make a Pudden; and has just Wit enough to know her Husband's Breeches from another Man's.

> 'Wit enough to know ...' : neither proverb nor catch-phrase, but another example of Sir John's earthy humour.

Lady Sm. My Lord *Sparkish,* I have some excellent Cyder, will you please to taste it.

> 'Cyder' : a spelling common since the 16th century; in the 20th, either a manufacturers' convention or a customer's affectation.

Lord Sp. My Lord, I should like it well enough, if it were not so treacherous.
Lord Sm. Pray, my Lord, how is it treacherous?
Lord Sp. Because it smiles in my Face, and cuts my Throat.

> 'how is it treacherous? – *Lord Sp.* Because it smiles in my Face, and cuts my Throat' : a 17th–19th (?20th) century proverb, apparently referring to the fact that it looks attractive but is much stronger than it looks.

[Here a loud Laugh.]
Miss. Odd so, Madam, your Knives are very sharp, for I have cut my Finger.
Lady Sm. I'm sorry for it, pray which Finger?
Miss. Why, this Finger, (God bless the Mark) no, 'tis this : I vow, I can't find which it is.

> 'God bless the Mark' : a genteel oath, comparable to 'God bless my soul !'

130

Nev. Ay, the Fox had a Wound, and he could not tell where, &c. Bring some Water to throw in her Face.

> 'the Fox had a Wound ... &c.' : with variants 'The fox was sick' and 'he knew not where', this is a 17th–19th century proverb. Neverout's '&c.' = 'He clapped his hand on his tail and swore it was there'. Apperson.
> 'Bring some water ...' : implication, 'She has fainted'.

Miss. Pray, Mr. *Neverout,* did you ever draw a Sword in Anger? I warrant, you would faint at the Sight of your own Blood.

> 'Did you ever draw a Sword in Anger?' : a studied insult.

Lady Sm. Mr. *Neverout,* shall I send you some Veal?
Nev. No, Madam, I don't love it.
Miss. Then, pray for them that do. I desire your Ladyship will send me a Bit.

> 'Then, pray for them that do' : 'Well, others do' phrased very politely.

Lord Sm. Tom, my Service to you.

> 'Tom, my Service to you' : I drink to you – 'I looks towards you'.

Nev. My Lord; this Moment, I did my self the Honour to drink to your Lordship.
Lord Sm. Why then, that's *Hartfordshire* Kindness.

> 'Hartfordshire Kindness' : Hertfordshire kindness = a drinking twice to the same person. Current *c.* 1650–1900.

Lord Sp. Why then, Colonel, my humble Service to you.
Nev. Pray, my Lord, don't make a Bridge of my Nose.

> 'don't make a Bridge of my Nose' : don't pass me over, don't pass me by, in drinking : common in mid-17th–19th century, then rare.

Lord Sp. Well, a Glass of this Wine is as comfortable, as Matrimony to an old Maid.

> 'as comfortable, as Matrimony to an old Maid' : an ambiguous saying, for matrimony, although welcome, may be very uncomfortable to one.

Col. Sir *John,* I design one of these Days, to come and beat up your Quarters in *Derbyshire.*

> 'beat up your Quarters' : pay you an unexpected, or unceremonious, visit. A colloquialism, the literal sense being 'arouse' or 'disturb'. The Colonel affects the jargon of his profession.

Sir John. Faith, Colonel, come and welcome; and stay away, and heartily welcome. But you were born within the Sound of *Bow* Bell, and don't Care to stir so far from *London*.

> 'come and welcome; and stay away, and heartily welcome': a mild adaptation of 'Come and welcome, go by and no quarrel' (mid-17th–mid-19th century).
> 'born within the Sound of *Bow* Bell': a late 16th–20th century description – since *c.* 1850, usually 'Bow bells' – of a true Cockney. The bell or bells hang within the steeple of Bow Church in Cheapside; a church destroyed during World War II and restored *c.* 1960.

Miss. Pray, Colonel, send me some Fritters.

> [*Colonel takes them out with his Hand.*]

Col. Here, Miss, they say, Fingers were made before Forks, and Hands before Knives.

> 'Fingers were made before Forks, and Hands before Knives': goes back to *c.* 1550. In the 19th–20th centuries, the latter half has usually been omitted.

Lady Sm. Methinks, this Pudden is too much boyl'd.

Lady Answ. O, Madam, they say a Pudden is Poison, when it's too much boyl'd.

> 'a Pudden is Poison, when it's too much boyl'd': a culinary proverb or, perhaps rather, a piece of culinary folklore. Recorded only by Swift?

Nev. Miss, shall I help you to a Pigeon? Here's a Pigeon so finely roasted, it cries, Come eat me.

> 'so finely roasted, it cries, Come eat me': Tom grows lyrical.

Miss. No, Sir, I thank you.

Nev. Why then, you may chuse.

Miss. I have chosen already.

Nev. Well; you may be worse offered, before you are twice married.

> 'you may be worse offered, before . . .': you may be offered worse fare . . .

> [*The Colonel fills a large Plate of Soupe.*]

Lord Sm. Why, Colonel, you don't mean to eat all that Soupe?

> 'Soupe': the French spelling was common throughout the 17th–18th centuries.

Col. O, my Lord, this is my sick Dish; when I am well, I have a Bigger.

> 'my sick Dish; . . . a Bigger': what I eat when not feeling very well.

Miss. [*To Colonel.*] Sup *Simon;* good Broth.

'Sup *Simon;* good Broth' : with several slight variants, current throughout the 17th–19th centuries; in the 19th, mainly rural. An ironic catch-phrase.

Nev. This seems to be a good Pullet.

Miss. I warrant, Mr. *Neverout*, knows what's good for himself.

Lord Sp. Tom, I shan't take your Word for it, help me to a Wing.
[*Neverout tries to cut off a Wing.*]

Nev. I'gad, I can't hit the Joynt.

Lord Sp. Why then, think of a Cuckold.

Nev. O, now I have nickt it.

'I can't hit the Joynt . . . think of a Cuckold . . . now I have nickt it' : the second reference to the saying 'Think of a cuckold' as applied to meat difficult to joint, the other being 'If a cuckold come, he'll take away' – or 'run away with' – 'the meat' : 17th–mid-19th centuries. Apperson quotes an anecdotal origin.

[*Gives it Lord* Sparkish.]

Lord Sp. Why, a Man may eat this, though his Wife lay a Dying.

'a Man may eat this . . .' : it's wonderfully good.

Col. Pray, Friend, give me a Glass of Small-Beer, if it be good.

Lord Sm. Why, Colonel, they say, there is no such Thing as good Small-Beer, good brown Bread, or a good old Woman.

'there is no such thing as . . .' : apparently a late 17th–18th century proverb. (*ODEP.*)

Lady Sm. [*To Lady* Answerall.] Madam, I beg your Ladyship's Pardon, I did not see you when I was cutting that Bit.

Lady Answ. O, Madam, after you is good Manners.

'after you is good Manners' : 'After you' is . . . : 17th–19th century. Kelly, 1721, notes that it is 'spoken when our betters offer to serve us first'.

Lady Sm. Lord, here's a Hair in the Sawce.

Lord Sp. Then, Madam, set the Hounds after it.

'a Hair in the Sawce . . . set the Hounds after it' : hair, hare, ha! ha!

Nev. Pray, Colonel, help me, however, to some of that same Sawce.

Col. Come, I think you are more Sawce than Pig.

'you are more Sawce than Pig' : impudent rather than greedy : 17th–18th centuries.

Lord Sm. Sir *John*, chear up, my Service to you : Well, what do you think of the World to come?

Sir John. Truly, my Lord, I think of it as little as I can.

> 'chear up' : 'Cheer up!' The spelling *chear* belongs to the 16th–18th centuries.
>
> 'What do you think . . .?' : Sir John's reply, '. . . as little as I can' is agreeably witty. It is well to remember that, for all his bluff outspokenness, the man was nobody's fool.

Lady Sm. [*Putting a Skewer on a Plate.*] Here, take this Skewer, and carry it down to the Cook, to dress it for her own Dinner.

> 'Here, take this Skewer . . . for her own Dinner' : a time-honoured jest between a 'character' and her cook, or so I suppose.

Nev. I beg your Ladyship's Pardon; but this Small-Beer is dead.

Lady Sm. Why then, let it be bury'd.

> 'this Small-Beer is dead. – Why then, let it be bury'd' : small beer – here, probably, weak (rather than inferior) beer – naturally tends to go 'dead' (lifeless) or flat. Her Ladyship is in a playful mood.

Col. This is admirable black Pudden; Miss, shall I carve you some? I am the worst Carver in the World; I should never make a good Chaplain. I can just carve Pudden, and that's all.

> 'the worst Carver in the World; . . . never make a good Chaplain' : a chaplain attached to a great house was expected to carve the meat at table.

Miss. No, thank ye, Colonel; for they say, those that eat black Pudden, will dream of the Devil.

> 'those that eat black Pudden . . .' : apparently recorded first, and only, by Swift.

Lord Sm. O, here comes the Venison Pasty: Here, take the Soupe away.

> [*He cuts it up, and tastes the Venison.*]

S'buds, this Venison is musty.

> ' 'S'buds' : an oath, shortened from (*God*)'s *bodikins* and current *c.* 1650-1800.

> [Neverout *eats a Piece, and burns his Mouth.*]

Lord Sm. What's the Matter, *Tom?* You have Tears in your Eyes, I think. What dost cry for, Man?

Nev. My Lord, I was just thinking of my poor Grandmother; she dyed just this very Day seven Years.

> 'I was thinking of my poor Grandmother' : an ancient excuse – even older than that of attendance at her funeral. Miss comes in, nicely on cue; and Lord Smart very properly, if rather conventionally, applauds her wit.

[Miss takes a Bit, and burns her Mouth.]

Nev. And pray, Miss, why do you cry too?

Miss. Because you were not hanged the Day your Grandmother dyed.

Lord Sm. I'd have given forty Pounds, Miss, to have said that.

Col. I'gad, I think, the more I eat, the hungryer I am.

> 'the more I eat . . .': another tune on the theme of 'l'appétit vient en mangeant'.

Lord Sp. Why, Colonel, they say, one Shoulder of Mutton drives down another.

> 'one Shoulder of Mutton . . .': recorded by Ray in 1670 and used, allusively, by Tennyson in 1833 (*ODEP*). Now rare.

Nev. I'gad, if I were to fast for my Life, I would take a good Break-fast in the Morning, a good Dinner at Noon, and a good Supper at Night.

> 'if I were to fast . . .': mid-17th–early 19th century. Ray, 1678.

Lord Sp. My Lord, this Venison is plaguily pepper'd. Your Cook has a heavy Hand.

> 'plaguily': excessively.

Lord Sm. My Lord, I hope you are Pepper Proof. Come, here's a Health to the Founders.

Lady Sm. Ay, and to the Confounders too.

> 'a Health to the Founders': originally (and still) a genuine health, it had apparently become a sort of catch-phrase substituted for a specific health.
>
> 'and to the Confounders too': no particular reference, I think. A pun: to those who cause confusion.

Lord Sm. Lady *Answerall*, does not your Ladyship love Venison?

Lady Answ. No, my Lord, I can't endure it in my Sight; therefore please to send me a good Piece of Meat and Crust.

Lord Sp. [*Drinks to* Neverout.] Come, *Tom*, not always to my Friends, but once to you.

Nev. [*Drinks to Lady* Smart.] Come, Madam, here's a Health to our Friends, and hang the rest of our Kin.

> 'not always to my Friends, but once to you . . . a Health to our Friends, and hang the rest of our Kin': jocose, punning toasts of the same order as the 20th century (and earlier?): 'To those who like us and others like us!'

Lady Sm. [*To Lady* Answerall.] Madam, will your Ladyship have any of this Hare?

Lady Answ. No, Madam; they say 'tis melancholy Meat.

Lady Sm. Then, Madam, shall I send you the Brains: I beg your Ladyship's Pardon, for they say, 'tis not good Manners to offer Brains.

'. . . Hare? . . . 'tis melancholy Meat': folklore declaring, 16th century onwards, that eating the flesh of hares causes melancholy. 'not good Manners to offer Brains': the implication being, of course, that the prospective recipient has none or, at the least, not enough. Social folklore.

Lady Answ. No, Madam, for perhaps it will make me Hare-brain'd.

'Hare-brain'd': having no more brains than a hare; heedless. Mid-16th–20th centuries.

Nev. Miss, I must tell you one Thing.

Miss. [*With a Glass in her Hand.*] Hold your Tongue, Mr. *Neverout;* don't speak in my Tip.

'in my Tip': into my glass; as I am busy drinking. Short for *tipple*? Long obsolete.

Col. Well, he was an ingenious Man that first found out eating and drinking.

Lord Sp. Of all Vittels, Drink digests the quickest. Give me a Glass of Wine.

'Of all Vittels . . .': with variants 'meat' (nourishment) for 'victuals' and 'goes down the best' for 'digests the quickest', this proverb apparently dates from late 17th century and is still heard occasionally.

Nev. My Lord, your Wine is too strong.

Lord Sm. Ay, *Tom,* as much as you are too good.

'your Wine . . . too good': no more too strong than you too good – not at all.

Miss. This Almond Pudden was pure good; but it is grown quite cold.

'pure good': couldn't be better.

Nev. So much the better Miss; cold Pudden will settle your Love.

'cold Pudden will settle your Love': mid-17th–19th century general; mid-19th–20th, rural. Here, *settle* = to calm, to allay.

Miss. Pray, Mr. *Neverout,* are you going to take a Voyage?

Nev. Why, do you ask, Miss?

Miss. Because, you have laid in so much Beef.

'laid in so much Beef' : taken it aboard; in short, consumed, eaten.

Sir John. You two have eat up the whole Pudden betwixt you.

Miss. Sir *John,* here's a little Bit left, will you please to have it?

Sir John. No, thankee, I don't love to make a Fool of my Mouth.

'. . . make a Fool of my Mouth' : I couldn't be bothered – there's so little.

Col. [*Calling to the Butler.*] John, is your Small-Beer good?

Butler. An please your Honour, my Lord and Lady like it; I think it is good.

'An please your Honour' : if it please you, Sir. By 1738, indeed by 1700, *an* for 'if' was already archaic. In dialect, it survived well into the 19th century.

Col. Why then, *John,* d'ye see, if you are sure your Small-Beer is good, d'ye mark? Then give me a Glass of Wine. [*All laugh.*]

Lady Sm. Sir *John,* how does your Neighbour *Gatherall* of the Park? I hear he has lately made a Purchase.

Sir John. Oh; *Dick Gatherall* knows how to butter his Bread, as well as any Man in *Derbyshire.*

'knows how to butter his Bread' : an allusion to the 16th–20th century proverbial phrase, 'to know on which side his bread is buttered'.

Lady Sm. Why he used to go very fine, when he was here in Town.

'go very fine' : to live well and dress very fashionably or elegantly. The phrase did not long survive the 18th century.

Sir John. Ay, and it became him, as a Saddle becomes a Sow.

'it became him . . .' : the style suited him as badly as a saddle does a sow : 16th–mid-19th century, general; then rural.

Col. I knew his Lady; and, I think, she's a very good Woman.

Sir John. Faith, she has more Goodness in her little Finger, than he has in his whole Body.

'more Goodness in her little Finger . . .' : one form of the thought-pattern usually taken to have been indicated by the 18th–20th century 'to have more wit in one's little finger than another has in his whole body'.

[*Colonel tasting the Wine.*]

Lord Sm. Well, Colonel, how do you like that Wine?

Col. This Wine should be eaten; 'tis too good to be drank.

'This Wine should be eaten . . .' : it has such body and such flavour. Not, one supposes, original to the Colonel; probably a catch-phrase.

Lord Sm. I'm very glad you like it; and, pray don't spare it.

Col. No, my Lord; I'll never starve in a Cook's Shop.

'I'll never starve in a Cook's Shop' (an eating-house) : I have too much sense to starve amid plenty : 17th–18th century.

Lady Sm. And, pray Sir *John,* what do you say to my Wine?

Sir John. I'll take another Glass first : Second Thoughts are best.

'Second Thoughts are best' : 16th–20th centuries. Greek and Latin prototypes.

Lord Sp. Pray, Lady *Smart,* you sit near that Ham, will you please to send me a Bit?

Lady Sm. With all my Heart. [*She sends him a Piece.*] Pray, my Lord, how do you like it?

Lord Sp. I think it is a Limb of *Lot's* Wife. [*He eats it with Mustard.*] I'gad, my Lord, your Mustard is very uncivil.

'a Limb of *Lot's* Wife' : (very) salty, Lot's wife having been turned into pillar of salt.

'Mustard very uncivil' : so hot and sharp that it takes him by the nose. Compare the simile, 'as keen as mustard'.

Lady Sm. Why uncivil, my Lord?

Lord Sp. Because, it takes me by the Nose, I'gad.

Lady Sm. Mr. *Neverout,* I find you are a very good Carver.

Col. Oh Madam, that's no Wonder; for you must know, *Tom Neverout* carves a-Sundays.

'carves a-Sundays' : on Sundays. This overt statement contains, I feel sure, a covert witticism – but I don't recognize it.

[*Mr.* Neverout *overturns the Saltcellar.*]

Lady Sm. Mr. *Neverout,* you have overturn'd the Salt; and that's a Sign of Anger. I'm afraid Miss and you will fall out.

'overturn'd the Salt; . . . a sign of Anger' : a bad omen, the usual implication being of a quarrel or especially a misfortune, avertible by casting some of the spilt salt over the left shoulder. Compare the next note. Compare also the 17th–20th century proverb, 'Help one to salt, help one to sorrow'.

Lady Answ. No, no; throw a little of it into the Fire, and all will be well.

'throw a little of it into the Fire' : obsolescent as a remedy, there being so few open fires.

Nev. O Madam, the falling *out* of Lovers, you know——
Miss. Lovers! very fine! fall *out* with him! I wonder when we were *in.*

> 'fall *out* with him! I wonder . . .' : *fall out,* to disagree or even to quarrel, goes back to *c.* 1550 or earlier.

Sir John. For my Part, I believe the young Gentlewoman is his Sweet-Heart; there's such fooling and fidling betwixt them. I am sure, they say in our Country, that shiddle come sh——'s the Beginning of Love.

> 'shiddle come sh——'s the Beginning of Love' : the proverb does not appear in the two best-known collections. The phrase *shiddle come shit* is obscure, *shiddle* failing to have qualified for Joseph Wright's wonderful *English Dialect Dictionary;* nor does it occur in either of the *Two Collections of Derbicisms,* made by the Rev Samuel Pegge (1704–96) late in life. Tentatively I suggest that it is a variant of *shittle,* itself a dialectal variant of *shuttle,* which, as verb, has a sense 'to dart backwards and forwards' as a shuttle does – hence, to waver; the adjective *shittle* = variable, wavering, inconstant. One feels tempted to relate *shiddle come shit* to *shilly-shally,* recorded by the *OED* for 1703, or, rather, to the original *shill I, shall I* occurring in 1700.

Miss. Nay, I love Mr. *Neverout,* as the Devil loves holy Water. I love him like Pye, I'd rather the Devil wou'd have him than I.

> 'as the Devil loves holy Water' : recorded by Ray, 1678 : a variant of the 16th–17th century 'The Devil loves no holy water'. Sense: I detest him.
> 'I love him like Pye . . . than I' : the rhyming clause is supplied by Miss; the other part forms an allusion to the 17th–18th century 'I love thee like pudding, if thou wert pie I'd eat thee'.

Nev. Miss, I'll tell you one thing.
Miss. Come, here's t'ye to stop your Mouth.

> 'here's t'ye to stop your Mouth' : Here's a health to you, to stop you from talking.

Nev. I'd rather you would stop it with a Kiss.
Miss. A Kiss; marry come up my dirty Couzin : Are you no sicker? Lord! I wonder what Fool it was, that first invented kissing?

> 'marry come up my dirty Couzin : Are you no sicker?' Halliwell, 1847, remarks of 'Marry! come up, my dirty cousin' – occurring first in 1674 – that it is 'a saying addressed to any one who affects excessive modesty'. Here, it seems that Miss kisses Tom and then asks 'Are you . . .?'

Nev. Well, I'm very dry.

Miss. Then you are the better to burn, and the worse to fry.

'Well, I'm very dry . . . the worse to fry' : a crambo.

Lady Answ. God bless you, Colonel, you have a good Stroak with you.

'you have a good Stroak with you' : you're a notable trencherman.

Col. O Madam, formerly I could eat all, but now I leave nothing; I eat but one Meal a-Day.

Miss. What? I suppose, Colonel, that's from Morning till Night.

'formerly I could eat all, but now I leave nothing . . . from Morning till Night' : the Colonel apparently quotes a catch-phrase and Miss apparently is being original.

Nev. Faith, Miss, and well was his Want.

'well was his Want' : ? he wanted much; or ? his wants (desires) were seemly.

Lord Sm. Pray, Lady *Answerall*, taste this Bit of Venison.

Lady Answ. I hope, your Lordship, will set me a good Example.

Lord Sm. Here's a Glass of Cyder fill'd. Miss, you must drink it.

Miss. Indeed, my Lord, I can't.

Nev. Come Miss; better Belly burst than good Liquor be lost.

'better Belly burst than . . .' : with variants 'drinks' for 'liquor', recorded as early as 1659; with variant 'meat' as early as 1678 and as late as 1917. Since *c.* 1800, mainly rural. (Apperson; *ODEP.*)

Miss. Pish, well, in Life there was never any Thing so teazing; I had rather shed it in my Shoes : I wish it were in your Guts, for my Share.

'shed it in my Shoes' : pour it into them.

'I wish it were . . . for my Share' : so far as my share goes, you're welcome to it. Miss can, under provocation, be almost as coarse as Tom seems to delight in being.

Lord Sm. Mr. *Neverout,* you ha'n't tasted my Cyder yet.

Nev. No, my Lord, I have been just eating Soupe; and they say, if one drinks in one's Porridge, one will cough in one's Grave.

'if one drinks . . . Grave' : mid-17th–mid-19th century. Early variant : pottage.

Lord Sm. Come, take Miss's Glass, she wish't it was in your Guts; let her have her Wish for once; Ladies can't abide to have their Inclinations cross't.

Lady Sm. [*To Sir* John.] I think, Sir *John,* you have not tasted the Venison yet.

Sir John. I seldom eat it, Madam : However, please to send me a little of the Crust.

Lord Sp. Why, Sir *John,* you had as good eat the Devil, as the Broth he's boyl'd in.

> 'you had as good eat the Devil . . .' : 15th–20th centuries; since late 19th, mostly rural. *Si peccas, pecca fortiter.*

Nev. I have dined as well as my Lord-Mayor.

> 'dined as well as my Lord-Mayor' : often in full ('. . . of London'), this saying goes back to the 16th century and fell into disuse only *c.* 1890. A reference to official banquets at the predecessors of the Mansion House (built 1739 – 1753).

Miss. I thought I could have eaten this Wing of a Chicken; but, I find, my Eye's bigger than my Belly.

> 'my Eye's bigger than my Belly' : occurs in Lyly's *Euphues and His England,* 1580. Since *c.* 1850, usually 'eyes bigger than one's stomach'.

Lord Sm. Indeed, Lady *Answerall,* you have eaten nothing.

Lady Answ. Pray, my Lord, see all the Bones on my Plate. They say, a Carpenter's known by his Chips.

> 'a Carpenter's known by his Chips', occurring in Coryat's *Crudities,* 1611, extends the pithy 'Such *or* like carpenter, such *or* like chips', occurring in Heywood, 1546. (Apperson; *ODEP.*) The origin of the inseparable nick-name 'Chips' for all Carpenters.

Nev. Miss, will you reach me that Glass of Jelly?

Miss. [*Giving it to him.*] You see, 'tis but ask and have.

> ' 'tis but ask and have' : you have only to ask in order to get it.

Nev. Miss, I would have a bigger Glass.

Miss. What, you don't know your own Mind; you are neither well full nor fasting. I think that is enough.

> 'neither well full nor fasting' = well, neither full nor fasting = satisfied . . . The original is : 'Never well, full nor fasting', with variant 'pleased' for 'well' : 17th (probably mid-16th)–20th centuries; latterly, mostly rural.

Nev. Ay, one of the enough's : I am sure it is little enough.

> 'one of the enough's' : the other being 'quite enough'.

Miss. Yes, but you know sweet Things are bad for the Teeth.

'sweet Things . . .': goes back to Dekker, 1607, and probably much further.

Nev. [*To Lady* Answerall.] Madam, I don't like this Part of the Veal you sent me.

Lady Answ. Well, Mr. *Neverout,* I find you are a true *English*-Man, you never know when you are well.

'a true *English*-Man . . .': always grumbling, as is (he thinks) his privilege. Compare 'neither well . . .' above.

Col. Well, I have made my whole Dinner of Beef.

Lady Ans. Why, Colonel, a Belly full is a Belly full, if it be but of Wheat-Straw.

'a Belly full . . . Wheat-Straw': a departure from the standard 'A bellyful is a bellyful, whether it be meat or drink' (mid-17th–19th centuries, ? 20th).

Col. Well, after all, Kitchen Physick is the best Physick.

'Kitchen Physick is the best Physic': 16th–19th centuries. Recorded in a dietary published in 1542. (*ODEP.*)

Lord Sm. And the best Doctors in the World, are Doctor *Diet,* Doctor *Quiet,* and Doctor *Merryman.*

'the best Doctors . . . are Doctor *Diet,* Doctor *Quiet,* and Doctor *Merryman*': occurs in Bulleyn's *Government of Health,* 1558, with 'physicians' for 'doctors', and the prescription is still recommended; sometimes 'Dr Brighton' is mentioned approvingly.

Lord Sp. What do you think of a little House well filled?

Sir John. And a little Land well till'd?

Col. Ay, and a little Wife well will'd?

'a little House well filled . . . till'd . . . will'd: a crambo. 'Well will'd' = well endowed by her father's (or uncle's or . . .) will.

Nev. My Lady *Smart,* pray help me to some of the Breast of that Goose.

Lord Sm. Tom, I have heard, that Goose upon Goose is false Heraldry.

'Goose upon Goose is false Heraldry': Lord Smart is playing upon the proverb, 'Metal upon metal is false heraldry' (17th–20th centuries), recorded by *ODEP.*

Miss. What! will you never have done stuffing?

Lord Sm. This Goose is quite raw. Well; God sends Meat, but the Devil sends Cooks.

'God sends Meat . . .': 16th–20th centuries; occasionally 'and' for 'but'.

Nev. Miss, can you tell which is the white Goose, or the grey Goose the Gander?

> 'which is the white Goose . . . the Gander?' : an example of that kind of question which admits of no answer, a 'trick question' – like (say) 'Which would you rather or go fishing?' Compare :

Miss. They say, a Fool will ask more Questions, than twenty wise Men can answer.

> 'a Fool will ask . . .' : the standard form is, 'A fool may ask more questions in an hour than a wise man can answer in seven years'; occasionally 'will' rather than 'may'. Mid-17th–20th centuries.

Col. Indeed, Miss, *Tom Neverout* has posed you.

> 'posed' : settled, got the better of, you.

Miss. Why, Colonel, every Dog has his Day. But, I believe, I shall never see a Goose again, without thinking on Mr. *Neverout*.

> 'every Dog has his Day' : 16th–20th centuries. A rural variant adds 'and a bitch two afternoons'.
> 'I shall never see a Goose without thinking on Mr *Neverout*': follows a conversational pattern (nowadays with 'of' for 'on'), 'Mr *Neverout*' being the sole variable.

Lord Sm. Well said Miss; I'faith Girl, thou hast brought thy self off cleverly. *Tom*, what say you to that?

> 'hast brought thy self off cleverly' : come out of the exchange with honours.

Col. Faith, *Tom* is nonplust; he looks plaguily down in the Mouth.

> 'down in the Mouth' : dejected or dispirited. In 17th–19th centuries, familiar Standard English; in the 20th, increasingly colloquial.

Miss. Why, my Lord, you see he's the provokingest Creature in Life : I believe, there is not such another in the varsal World.

> 'in the varsal World' : in the whole wide world. *Varsal,* a variant of the earlier *versal,* is a slightly illiterate colloquialism of the late 17th–18th centuries, and then obsolete except in dialect.

Lady Answ. Oh Miss, the World's a wide Place.

> 'the World's a wide Place' : aren't you rather exaggerating?

Nev. Well, Miss, I'll give you Leave to call me any Thing, so you don't call me Spade.

> 'any Thing, so you don't call me Spade' : provided you don't call me a eunuch. This rare word, noted by the *OED* for 1680, comes from Latin *spado.*

Lord Sm. Well, but after all, *Tom,* can you tell me what's *Latin* for a Goose?

Nev. O my Lord, I know that; Why, Brandy is *Latin* for a Goose; and *Tace* is *Latin* for a Candle.

> 'Brandy is *Latin* for a Goose; and *Tace* is Latin for a Candle': the 'Brandy . . .' part occurs as early as 1588 and appears in Halliwell, 1847, thus: *'Brandy is Latin for pig and goose,* an apology for drinking a dram after either'; and *'Tace . . .* Candle', occurring as early as 1676, is a hint to keep silent (Latin *Tace,* Be silent!). Both sayings are extant among the educated – but only just extant.

Miss. Is that Manners, to shew your Learning before Ladies? Methinks you are grown very brisk of a sudden. I think, the Man's glad he's alive.

> 'Is that Manners . . .?': or, come to that, before gentlemen. Perhaps a proverb, as *ODEP* adjudges it.

Sir John. The Devil take your Wit, if this be Wit: for it spoils Company. Pray, Mr. Butler, bring me a Dram after my Goose; 'tis very good for the Wholesoms.

> 'very good for the Wholesoms' = very wholesome. Normally, *wholesomes* means 'wholesome drinks, wholesome foods'; here, it is either slangy or dialectal.

Lord Sm. Come, bring me the Loaf; I sometimes love to cut my own Bread.

Miss. I suppose, my Lord, you lay longest a Bed to-Day.

Lord Sm. Miss, if I had said so, I should have told a Fib: I warrant you lay a Bed 'till the Cows came home. But, Miss, shall I cut you a little Crust, now my Hand is in?

> 'Fib': a colloquialism, noted by Cotgrave in 1611, and probably deriving from *fible-fable,* a reduplication of *fable.*
> 'lay a Bed 'till the Cows come home': the unit is *'til(l) the cows come home,* earliest (1610) *till the cow come home* (for milking).

Miss. If you please, my Lord; a Bit of under Crust.

Nev. [*Whispering Miss.*] I find you love to lie under.

> 'love to lie under': innuendo.

Miss. [*Aloud; pushing him from her.*] What does the Man mean? Sir, I don't understand you at all.

Nev. Come, all Quarrels laid aside: Here, Miss, may you live a thousand Years. [*He drinks to her.*]

Miss. Pray Sir, don't stint me.

Lord Sm. Sir *John,* will you taste my *October?* I think it is very good; but, I believe, not equal to yours in *Derbyshire.*

'will you taste my *October?*' : short for *October ale,* brewed in that month.

Sir John. My Lord, I beg your Pardon; but, they say, the Devil made Askers.

'the Devil made Askers' : apparently the earliest record of a proverb that never became very general.

Lord Sm. [*To the Butler.*] Here, bring up the great Tankard full of *October,* for Sir *John.*
Col. [*Drinking to Miss.*] Miss, your Health; may you live all the Days of your Life.

'may you live all the Days . . .' : live fully, not merely exist.

Lady Ans. Well, Miss, you'll certainly be soon married : Here's two Bachelors drinking to you at once.

'soon married' : partly an example of social folklore, partly a proverb.

Lady Sm. Indeed, Miss, I believe you were wrapt in your Mother's Smock, you are so well beloved.

'wrapt in your Mother's Smock' : born lucky. With occasional variant 'lapped' for 'wrapped', it dates from the latter 16th century; now rural.

Miss. Where's my Knife, sure I han't eaten it? O, here it is.
Sir John. No, Miss, but your Maidenhead hangs in your Light.

'your Maidenhead . . .' : virginity is to your disadvantage.

Miss. Pray, Sir *John,* is that a *Derbyshire* Compliment? Here, Mr. *Neverout,* will you take this Piece of Rabbit, that you bid me carve for you?

'Derbyshire compliment' : not an allusion, but a pointed idiosyncrasy, imputing coarseness.

Nev. I don't know.
Miss. Why, why, take it, or let it alone.
Nev. I will.
Miss. What will you?
Nev. Why, take it, or let it alone.
Miss. Well, you're a provoking Creature.
Sir John. [*Talking with a Glass of Wine in his Hand.*] I remember a Farmer in our Country——

Lord Sm. [*Interrupting him.*] Pray, Sir *John,* did you ever hear of Parson *Palmer?*

> 'Parson *Palmer* . . . used to preach over his Liquor' : a neat forestallment. Was he a 'character' of the day, or did Lord Smart tactfully invent him?

Sir John. No, my Lord, what of him?

Lord Sm. Why, he used to preach over his Liquor.

Sir John. I beg your Pardon. Here's your Lordship's Health; I'd drink it up, if it were a Mile to the Bottom.

> 'I'd drink it up . . .' : no matter how much there was in my glass.

Lady Sm. Mr. *Neverout,* have you been at the new Play?

Nev. Yes, Madam, I went the first Night.

Lady Sm. Well, and how did it take?

Nev. Why, Madam, the Poet is *damn'd.*

Sir John. God forgive you; that's very uncharitable; you ought not to judge so rashly of any Christian.

Nev. [*Whispers Lady* Smart.] Was ever such a Dunce? How well he knows the Town! see how he stares like a stuck Pig! Well, but Sir *John,* are you acquainted with any of our fine Ladies yet? Any of our famous Toasts?

> 'stares like a stuck Pig!' : mid-17th–20th century metaphor become a proverbial phrase.
> 'famous Toasts' : beauties much toasted by the men of London.

Sir John. No, damn your Fireships; I have a Wife of my own.

> 'Fireships' : slang of *c.* 1670–1770 for prostitutes, especially if diseased.

Lady Sm. Pray, my Lady *Answerall,* how do you like these preserved Oranges?

Lady Ans. Indeed, Madam, the only Fault I find, is, that they are too good.

Lady Sm. O, Madam, I have heard 'em say, that too good, is stark naught.

> 'too good, is stark naught' : too good is no good.

[*Miss drinking Part of a Glass of Wine.*]

Nev. Pray, let me drink your Snuff.

> 'let me drink your Snuff' : the remainder of your wine. Or so I guess, for I don't see what else it can mean.

Miss. No, indeed, you shan't drink after me; for you'll know my Thoughts.

'drink after me . . . Thoughts' : social folklore.

Nev. I know them already; you are thinking of a good Husband. Besides, I can tell your Meaning, by your Mumping.

'can tell your Meaning, by your Mumping' : by your grimacing. With variants 'winking' (rare) and 'gaping' (common), the saying was current *c.* 1620–1800.

Lady Sm. Pray, my Lord, did not you order the Butler to bring up a Tankard of our *October* to Sir *John?* I believe, they stay to brew it.

'they stay to brew it' : are waiting until they've brewed it. A thought-and-speech pattern represented nowadays by 'They must be *making* the thing !'

[*The Butler brings the Tankard to Sir* John.]

Sir John. Won't your Lordship please to drink first?

Lord Sm. No, Sir *John,* 'tis in a very good Hand : I'll pledge you.

Col. [*To Lord* Smart.] My Lord, I love *October* as well as Sir *John;* and I hope, you won't make Fish of one, and Flesh of another.

'make Fish of one, and Flesh of another' : discriminate unfairly, show partiality : *c.* 1620–1800 general; then rural.

Lord Sm. Colonel, you're heartily welcome : Come, Sir *John,* take it by Word of Mouth, and then give it the Colonel.

'take it by Word of Mouth' : drink it; don't talk – drink.

[*Sir* John *drinks.*]

Lord Sm. Well, Sir *John,* how do you like it?

Sir John. Not as well as my own in *Derbyshire.* 'Tis plaguy small.

'plaguy small' : very thin or weak. Compare *small*-beer.

Lady Sm. I never taste Malt Liquor; but they say, 'tis well Hopp'd.

'Malt Liquor . . . well Hopp'd' : with plenty of hops added.

Sir John. Hopp'd ! Why, if it had hopp'd a little further, it would have hopp'd into the River. O, my Lord; my Ale is Meat, Drink, and Cloth. It will make a Cat speak, and a wise Man dumb.

'hopp'd a little further . . . into the River' : compare milk watered at the parish pump.

'my Ale is Meat . . . a wise Man dumb' : 'Good ale is meat, drink, and cloth' goes back to the late 16th century, nor is it quite obsolete; and 'It will make a Cat speak, and a wise Man dumb' – in the simple form 'enough to make a cat speak' – occurs in *The Shirburn Ballads* (1585–1618) thus, 'Who is it but loves good liquor? 'Twill make a cat speak', and the full form occurs as early as 1661 in Ebsworth's *Antidote against Melancholy.* (Apperson.)

Lady Sm. I was told, ours was very strong.

Sir John. Ay, Madam, strong of the Water: I believe, the Brewer forgot the Malt, or the River was too near him. Faith, it is meer Whip-belly-vengeance: He that drinks most, has the worst Share.

> 'strong of the Water ... the Brewer forgot the Malt ...': Sir John belabours his point and then, to pile Pelion upon Ossa upon Olympus, describes his host's ale as 'meer Whip-belly-vengeance'; *w. – b. – v.,* perhaps first noted by Swift, is extant in dialect, has in Grose, 1788, the variant *pinch-gut vengeance,* and seems to elaborate the synonymous *rot-gut,* recorded in 1633 (*OED*). 'He that drinks most ...': could be Sir John's addition, although I doubt it.

Col. I believe, Sir *John,* Ale is as plenty as Water, at your House.

> 'as *plenty* as ...': the adjectival use of *plenty* is common in Middle English and indeed until *c.* 1850 – and then becomes colloquial rather than standard.

Sir John. Why, Faith, at Christmas we have many Comers and Goers; and they must not be sent away without a Cup of good *Christmas* Ale, for fear they should p—ss behind the Door.

> 'for fear that they should p–ss behind the Door': such urination being a rustic gesture of contempt for the niggardly.

Lady Sm. I hear, Sir *John* has the nicest Garden in *England;* they say, 'tis kept so clean, that you can't find a Place where to spit.

> 'the nicest Garden in *England*': an early, excellent, glaring example of the weakened, stop-gap use of *nice.*
> 'can't find a Place ...': an idiosyncratic rather than a commonplace expression.

Sir John. O, Madam, you are pleased to say so.

Lady Sm. But, Sir *John,* your Ale is terrible strong and heady in *Derbyshire;* and will soon make one drunk and sick, what do you then?

Sir John. Why, indeed, it is apt to Fox one; but our Way is, to take a Hair of the same Dog next Morning. I take a new laid Egg for Breakfast; and Faith, one should drink as much after an Egg, as after an Ox.

> 'is apt to Fox one': tends to make one drunk. This *fox* was originally (17th century) Standard English; in 19th–20th centuries, colloquial.
> 'to take a Hair of the same Dog': the dog that 'bit us' – the full form being 'a hair of the dog that bit me' (you, us, etc.) and current since early in the 16th century.
> 'one should drink as much ...': in 1608, Sir John Harington

quotes it in the form, 'For every egg you eat, you drink as oft'. Apparently obsolete, this proverb, was condemned by Ray as 'fond' – foolish – 'and ungrounded'.

Lord Sm. Tom Neverout, will you taste a Glass of the *October?*
Nev. No, Faith, my Lord, I like your Wine; and I won't put a Churl upon a Gentleman : Your Honour's Claret is good enough for me.

'put a Churl upon a Gentleman' : drink ale or beer immediately after wine, the implication being that ale is the drink of yokels, wine that of gentlemen. Recorded in 1576; apparently obsolete since *c.* 1850.

Lady Sm. What? is this Pigeon left for Manners? Colonel, shall I send you the Legs and Rump?
Col. Madam, I could not eat a Bit more, if the House was full.

'I could not eat a Bit more . . .' : even if the house were bulging with good things. (A mere guess.)

Lord Sm. [*Carving a Partridge.*] Well, one may ride to *Rumford* upon this Knife, it is so blunt.

'one may ride to Rumford . . .' (Romford, in Essex) : 18th–19th centuries. Why Romford? Merely for the alliteration, apparently.

Lady Answ. My Lord, I beg your Pardon; but they say, an ill Workman never had good Tools.

'an ill Workman never had good Tools' : usually 'An ill'– or, 19th–20th centuries, 'a bad' – 'workman quarrels with' – or 'blames' (or 'always blames') – his tools'. Since *c.* 1550.

Lord Sm. Will your Lordship have a Wing of it?
Lord Sp. No, my Lord, I love the Wing of an Ox a great deal better.

'the Wing of an Ox' : a shoulder of beef. Idiosyncratic, I suspect.

Lord Sm. I'm always cold after eating.
Col. My Lord, they say, that's a Sign of long Life.

'cold after eating . . . a Sign of long Life'. Compare : 'If you eat till you're cold, you'll live to grow old'.

Lord Sm. Ay, I believe I shall live 'till all my Friends are weary of me.
Col. Pray, does any Body here hate Cheese? I would be glad of a Bit.

'does any Body here hate Cheese?' : merely the Colonel's jocosity.

Lord Sm. An odd kind of Fellow dined with me t'other Day; and when the Cheese came upon the Table, he pretended to faint. So, some Body said, pray take away the Cheese : No, said I, pray take away the Fool : Said I well? [*Here a long and loud Laugh.*]

'An odd kind of Fellow . . . pray take away the Fool : Said I well?' : very well indeed, if it were his. But the anecdote sounds contrived. Perhaps compare *Twelfth Night* I, v, 34.

Col. Faith, my Lord, you served the Coxcomb right enough : And therefore, I wish we had a Bit of your Lordship's *Oxfordshire* Cheese.

'*Oxfordshire* cheese' : this mainly rural county has, for centuries, been noted for dairy-farming.

Lord Sm. Come, hang saving, bring us a halfporth of Cheese.

'hang saving, bring us a halfporth of Cheese' : a jocular catch-phrase rather than proverb : 17th–20th centuries. The form *half-porth* (better *half-p'orth*) is a clumsy reduction – contrast the phonetically and scripturally perfect *ha'p'orth* – of *halfpenny-worth*.

Lady Answ. They say, Cheese digests every Thing but itself.

'Cheese digests every Thing but itself' : late 16th–20th centuries; in the 20th, heard rarely except in the country. Ray, 1678, says 'This is a translation of that old rhyming Latin verse, *Caseus est nequàm, quia digerit omnia sequàm*' : Cheese is poor stuff, for it digests everything but itself.

[*Footman brings in a great whole Cheese.*]

Lord Sp. Ay, this would look handsome if any Body should come in.
Sir John. Well, I'm weily brosten, as they sayn in *Lancashire*.

'weily brosten' : well-nigh burst : *brosten* (for *bursten*) is a dialectal shape of the past participle *burst; weily* is a dialectal variant of *welly* (recorded in Pegge's *Derbicisms*), itself a dialectal contraction of *well nigh* or, rather, a corruption of *welny* (well nigh).

Lady Sm. Oh, Sir *John,* I wou'd I had something to brost you withal.
Lord Sm. Come, they say, 'tis merry in Hall, when Beards wag all.

' 'tis merry in Hall, when Beards wag all' : *ODEP* records it as having been used as early as *c.* 1300; common in 16th–18th centuries; rare in 19th; apparently obsolete by *c.* 1900.

Lady Sm. Miss, shall I help you to some Cheese? Or, will you carve for your self?
Nev. I'll hold fifty Pound, Miss won't cut the Cheese.

'I'll hold fifty Pound' : wager that sum.

Miss. Pray, why so, Mr. *Neverout?*

Nev. O, there is a Reason, and you know it well enough.

Miss. I can't, for my Life, understand what the Gentleman means.

Lord Sm. Pray, *Tom,* change the Discourse, in troth you are too bad.

> 'Oh, there is a Reason . . . I can't, for my Life, understand . . .
> Pray, *Tom,* change the Discourse . . .': here is some fashionable
> and apparently scabrous innuendo of the day. Perhaps a reference
> to 'Cheese won't choke her' (earliest as 'Cheese of three halfpence
> a pound': Tom Durfey, 1676): partly a proverbial saying and
> partly a catch-phrase, implying physical intimacy with men.

> [*Colonel whispers* Neverout.]

Col. Smoak Miss, you have made her fret like Gum taffety.

> 'fret like Gum taffety': usually '. . . gummed taffety' (taffeta) or
> occasionally, as in Shakespeare, 'velvet'. *ODEP* explains the pro-
> verbial saying, thus: 'the material being stiffened with gum,
> quickly rubbed and fretted itself out' (wore itself out).

Lady Sm. Well; but Miss, (hold your Tongue, Mr. *Neverout*) shall
I cut you a Bit of Cheese?

Miss. No really, Madam, I have dined this half Hour.

Lady Sm. What? quick at Meat, quick at work, they say.

> 'quick at Meat, quick at work': working well and eating fast:
> 17th–18th centuries and maybe later.

> [*Sir* John *nods.*]

Lord Sm. What, you are sleepy Sir *John.* Do you sleep after Dinner?

Sir John. Yes, Faith, I sometimes take a Nap after my Pipe; for
when the Belly's full, the Bones will be at rest.

> 'when the Belly's full, the Bones . . .': with variant 'would' for
> 'will', the proverb goes back to the 15th century; apparently obso-
> lete by 1900.

Lady Sm. Come, Colonel, help your self, and your Friends will love
you the better.

> [*To Lady* Answerall.]

Madam, your Ladyship eats nothing.

> 'help your self, and your Friends . . .': perhaps a reference to the
> 16th–20th century proverb, based on Greek and Latin : 'God helps
> them that help themselves'. This modern form seems to have been
> established, in 1736, by Benjamin Franklin.

Lady Answ. Lord, Madam, I have fed like a Farmer; I shall grow
as fat as a Porpoise: I swear, my Jaws are weary with chawing.

> 'I have fed like a Farmer': a 17th–18th century proverbial simile.

'as fat as a Porpoise' : late 17th–19th century. Much less common than '. . . as a pig'.

'chawing' : *chaw,* nowadays mainly dialectal, was reputable in the 16th–early 18th centuries as a variant of *chew.*

Col. I have a Mind to eat a Piece of that Sturgeon, but I fear it will make me sick.

Nev. A rare Soldier indeed; let it alone, and I warrant, it won't hurt you.

'a rare Soldier indeed' : the sturgeon has 'armour' (scutes or plates) rather like that of a soldier. Note, too, that in 1703 Dampier said of the red gurnard, known familiarly as a soldier fish, that it was 'mail'd somewhat like a Sturgeon' (*OED*).

'let it alone and . . . it won't hurt you' : perhaps a deliberate variation of the proverbial 'Let well alone'.

Col. Well, but it would vex a Dog to see a Pudden creep.

'it would vex a Dog to see a Pudden creep' : recorded first by Howell in 1659 and apparently obsolete by 1800.

[Sir John rises.]

Lord Sm. Sir *John,* what are you doing?

Sir John. Swolks, I must be going, by'r Lady; I have earnest Business; I must do, as the Beggars do, go away when I have got enough.

'Swolks' and 'by'r Lady' : oaths of the period, the latter (mid-16th–18th centuries, general; then rural) for *by our Lady;* the former, not very general, 'apparently a meaningless perversion of *Swounds*' (*OED*).

'as the Beggars do, go away . . .' : Sir John speaks from his experience of rural beggars.

Lord Sm. Well, but stay 'till this Bottle's out: You know, the Man was hanged that left his Liquor behind him; besides, a Cup in the Pate, is a Mile in the Gate; and, a Spur in the Head, is worth two in the Heel.

'the Man was hang'd that left . . .' : a 17th–mid-19th century proverb.

'a Cup in the Pate, is a Mile in the Gate' : a cup of wine inside one is worth a mile of one's journey : mid 17th–18th century. *Gate,* a going, a journey, a road, has become dialectal.

'a Spur in the Head . . .' : Ray, 1670. Kelly, 1721, explains that 'a man when drunk rides hard'. Apparently obsolete by 1900.

Sir John. Come then, one Brimmer to all your Healths.

[The Footman gives him a Glass half full.]

Pray, Friend, what was the rest of this Glass made for? An Inch at the Top, Friend, is worth two at the Bottom.

[*He gets a Brimmer, and drinks it off.*]

Well; there's no Deceit in a Brimmer; and there's no false Latin in this, your Wine is excellent good, so I thank you for the next; for, I am sure of this. Madam, has your Ladyship any Commands in *Derbyshire?* I must go fifteen Miles To-Night.

> 'one Brimmer' : one (preferably large) glass full to the brim.
> 'an Inch at the Top . . .' : Sir John's own, perhaps. Its witty 'nonsense logic' reminds me of (I think it was) Alexander Woollcott's 'It's not my first editions which are rare, but my second'.
> 'no false Latin in this' : a parting thrust at Tom Neverout for his 'Brandy is *Latin* for a Goose' of a few pages back.
> 'excellent good' : *excellent* = excellently = extremely.

Lady Sm. None, Sir *John,* but to take Care of yourself; and my most humble Service to your Lady unknown.

Sir John. Well, Madam, I can but love and thank you.

> 'I can but love and thank you' : *Mais que vous êtes galant, Monsieur!*

Lady Sm. Here, bring Water to wash; though really you have all eaten so little, that you have no Need to wash your Mouths.

Lord Sm. But prithee, Sir *John,* stay a while longer.

Sir John. No, my Lord, I am to smoak a Pipe with a Friend, before I leave the Town.

Col. Why, Sir *John,* had not you better set out To-morrow?

Sir John. Colonel, you forget, To-morrow is *Sunday.*

Col. Now, I always love to begin a Journey on Sundays, because I shall have the Prayers of the Church; to preserve all that Travel by Land or by Water.

> 'love to begin a Journey on Sundays . . . the Prayers of the Church' : for those in peril by land and sea.

Sir John. Well, Colonel, thou art a mad Fellow to make a Priest of.

> 'a mad Fellow to make a Priest of' : such words come strangely from you.

Nev. Fye, Sir *John,* do you take Tobacco? How can you make a Chimney of your Mouth?

> 'make a Chimney of your Mouth' : compare the 19th–20th century colloquialism 'to smoke like a chimney' (of a heavy smoker).

Sir John. [*To* Neverout.] What? you don't smoak, I warrant you, but you smock. (Ladies, I beg your Pardon.) Colonel, do you never smoke?

'but you smock' : fornicate. A phonetic pun. Not such a fool, our Derbyshire squire.

Col. No, Sir *John,* but I take a Pipe sometimes.

'do you never smoke?' – 'No, . . . but I take a Pipe sometimes' : a mocking reference to a genteelism of that day.

Sir John. I'Faith, one of your finical *London* Blades dined with me last year in *Derbyshire:* So, after Dinner, I took a Pipe : So, my Gentleman turn'd away his Head : So, said I, what Sir, do you never smoak? So, he answered as you do, Colonel, no; but I sometimes take a Pipe : So, he took a Pipe in his Hand, and fiddled with it, 'till be broke it : So, said I, pray, Sir, can you make a Pipe? So, he said, no : So, said I, why then, Sir, if you can't make a Pipe, you should not break a Pipe. So, we all laught.

'finical *London* Blades' : affected and fastidious young men-about-town.

Lord Sm. Well, but Sir *John,* they say that the Corruption of Pipes, is the Generation of Stoppers.

'the Corruption of Pipes, is the Generation of Stoppers' : this parody of the Latin philosophical maxim, *Corruptio unius, generatio alterius,* 'The corruption of one is the generation of another' (recorded for 1576), seems to mean 'The corruption exercised by' – hence, the popularity of – 'tobacco has led to the making of pipe-stoppers' (small devices for pressing the tobacco in one's pipe).

Sir John. Colonel, I hear you go sometimes to *Derbyshire,* I wish you would come and foul a Plate with me.

'foul a Plate with me' : share a meal.

Col. I hope, you'll give me a Soldier's Bottle.

'a Soldier's bottle' : a large one.

Sir John. Come, and try.

Sir John. Mr. *Neverout,* you are a Town-Wit, can you tell me what Kind of Herb is Tobacco?

Nev. Why, an *Indian* Herb, Sir *John.*

Sir John. No, 'tis a Pot-Herb; and so here's t'ye in a Pot of my Lord's *October.*

'a Pot-Herb; and so here's t'ye in a Pot . . .' : a tortured pun, for the tobacco plant is in no sense a pot-herb (kitchen-garden herb).

Lady Sm. I hear, Sir *John,* since you are married, you have forsworn the Town.

Sir John. No, Madam, I never forswore any Thing but building of Churches.

'never forswore any Thing . . .' : Sir John's own witticism, I suspect.

Lady Sm. Well, but Sir *John,* when may we hope to see you again in *London?*

Sir John. Why, Madam, not 'till the Ducks have eat up the Dirt, as the Children say.

'not 'till the Ducks . . .' : not until the (late) Spring. A rural saying.

Nev. Come, Sir *John,* I foresee it will rain terribly.

Lord Sm. Come, Sir *John,* do nothing rashly, let us drink first.

Lord Sp. Nay, I know Sir *John* will go, though he was sure it would rain Cats and Dogs. But, pray stay, Sir *John,* you'll be Time enough to go to Bed by Candle-light.

'rain Cats and Dogs' : rain violently. Probably since *c.* 1600.

Lord Sm. Why, Sir *John,* if you must needs go, while you stay, make good Use of your Time. Here's my Service to you. A Health to our Friends in *Derbyshire.*

Sir John. Not a Drop more.

Col. Why, Sir *John,* you used to love a Glass of good Wine in former Times.

Sir John. Why, so I do still, Colonel; but a Man may love his House very well, without riding on the Ridge; besides, I must be with my Wife on *Tuesday,* or there will be the Devil and all to pay.

'a man may love his House . . . Ridge' : the ridge or 'watershed' of the house. Either 'He does not need to go about proclaiming his love', or 'He may love it without ludicrous exaggeration'. The saying goes back to the 16th century; obsolete by 1900.

'the Devil and all to pay' : the very devil of an unbraiding, an extremely severe upbraiding : a late 17th–20th century colloquialism, perhaps originating in compacts with the Devil.

Col. Well, if you go To-Day, I wish you may be wet to the Skin.

Sir John. Ay, but they say, the Prayers of the Wicked won't prevail.

'the Prayers of the Wicked . . .' : *ODEP* classifies and quotes this as a proverb.

[*Sir* John *takes his Leave, and goes away.*]

Lord Sm. Well, Miss, how do you like Sir *John?*

Miss. Why, I think, he's a little upon the Silly, or so; I believe he has not all the Wit in the World; but I don't pretend to be a Judge.

'a little upon the silly' : a trifle silly, with 'silly' probably in the

sense 'simple-minded'. Nuance : He does rather *tend* to be . . .
'or so' : or something like that.

Nev. Faith, I believe he was bred at *Hogsnorton,* where the Pigs
play upon the Organs.

> 'bred at *Hogsnorton,* where the Pigs . . .' : usually written *Hogs
> Norton,* the place was mentioned as early as *c.* 1554 and the full
> statement made in 1593 by Nashe. (Apperson.) An arbitrary name,
> based on *King's* (etc.) *Norton* and using *Pigs* as an imputation of
> coarse rusticity – and revived, in the 1920s–1930s, by Mr Gillie
> Potter.

Lord Sp. Why, *Tom,* I thought you and he had been Hand and
Glove.

> 'had been hand and glove' : close friends : 17th–20th centuries.

Nev. Faith, he shall have a clean Threshold for me, I never darkned
his Door in my Life, neither in Town, nor Country; but, he's a queer
old Duke, by my Conscience; and yet, after all, I take him to be
more Knave than Fool.

> 'darkned his Door' : an 18th (? rather, late 17th–) 20th century
> phrase that has become a cliché.
> 'queer old Duke' : the unit is *queer duke,* a decayed gentleman : a
> late 17th–18th century term on the borderline of underworld cant
> and raffish fashionable slang.

Lord Sm. Well, come, a Man's a Man, if he has but a Hose on his
Head.

> ' a man's a man . . .' : for 'a that; no matter how oddly he may be
> dressed. A saying popular *c.* 1580–1780.

Col. I was once with him, and some other Company, over a Bottle;
and I'gad, he fell asleep, and snored so loud, that we thought he
was driving his Hogs to Market.

> 'snored so loud . . . driving his Hogs to Market' : the proverbial
> saying, which has variant 'pigs', has caused *drive one's hogs to
> market* to have the transferred sense, 'to snore'.

Nev. Why what? You can have no more of a Cat, than her Skin.
You can't make a Silk Purse out of a Sow's Ear.

> 'have no more of a Cat than her Skin' is synonymous with the
> ensuing 'can't make a silk Purse out of a Sow's Ear'. The former
> proverb, with variant 'but' for 'than', goes back to the 16th cen-
> tury – as also does the latter; the former is obsolescent.

Lord Sp. Well, since he's gone, the Devil go with him, and Sixpence;
and there's Money and Company too.

'the Devil go with him, and sixpence' : as a sort of viaticum.

Nev. Pray, Miss, let me ask you a Question?

Miss. Well, but don't ask Questions with a dirty Face. I warrant, what you have to say, will keep cold.

'don't ask Questions with a dirty Face' : either literally dirty after a huge meal or 'with a dirty look on your face'.

'what you have to say, will keep cold' : one rather suspects 'warm' or 'hot'; Miss perhaps implies 'will keep fresh' – 'won't go stale'.

Col. Come, my Lord, against you are disposed. Here's to all that love and honour you.

'against you are disposed' : while you are at hand and in the mood. The toast – with this or that word changed – is one of the neatest of the conventional healths.

Lord Sp. Ay, that was always *Dick Nimble*'s Health, I'm sure you know, he is dead.

Col. Dead! Well, my Lord, you love to be a Messenger of ill News, I'm heartily sorry; but, my Lord, we must all dye.

Nev. I knew him very well; but pray, how came he to dye?

Miss. There's a Question! You talk like a Poticary. Why, he dyed, because he could live no longer.

'Poticary' : a variant (since *c.* 1750, dialectal) of *pothecary,* aphetic for *apothecary.*

'He dyed, because . . . no longer' : which is something like saying 'He died of heart failure, as we all do'.

Nev. Well; rest his Soul; we must live by the Living, and not by the Dead.

'we must live by the Living . . .' : one suspects a pun on *by*=beside, with, and *by*=by means of. As a proverb, it dates since *c.* 1550 and usually has 'quick' for 'living'.

Lord Sp. You know his House was burnt down to the Ground.

Col. Yes, it was in the News. Why; Fire and Water are good servants, but they are very bad Masters.

'Fire and Water . . . Masters' : mostly without 'very', this proverb goes back at least as far as *c.* 1550.

Lord Sm. Here, take away, and set down a Bottle of Burgundy. Ladies, you'll stay and drink a Glass of Wine before you go to your Tea.

'a Bottle of Burgundy' : earliest English reference to this wine is Wycherley's 'honest Burgundy' in 1672 (*OED*).

[*All's taken away, and the Wine set down.*]
[*Miss gives* Neverout *a smart Pinch.*]

Nev. Lord, Miss, what d'ye mean? D'ye think I have no feeling?

Miss. I'm forced to pinch, for the Times are hard.

'forced to pinch, for the Times are hard' : a very neat pun on 'pinch and save'.

Nev. [*Giving Miss a Pinch.*] Take that, Miss: What's Sawce for a Goose, is Sawce for a Gander.

'Sawce for a Goose . . .' : Ray, 1670, shrewdly remarks, 'This is a woman's Proverb'.

Miss. [*screaming.*] Well, Mr. *Neverout,* if I live, that shall neither go to Heaven nor Hell with you.

'if I live, that shall . . .' : 'As I live' (intensive) – 'I shall go to neither Heaven nor Hell with you' (refuse to have anything to do with you).

Nev. [*takes Miss's Hand.*] Come, Miss, let us lay all Quarrels aside, and be Friends.

Miss. Don't be mauming and gauming a Body so. Can't you keep your filthy Hands to your self?

'mauming and gauming' : recorded only here, this phrase is a rhyming reduplication of *gaum,* to handle indelicately, itself recorded first in 1656. 'Don't paw!' The ensuing 'Can't you keep your filthy Hands to your self?' has a timeless ring.

Nev. Pray, Miss, where did you get that Pick-Tooth Case?

'that Pick-Tooth Case' : now *tooth-pick case.*

Miss. I came honestly by it.

Nev. I'm sure it was mine, for I lost just such a one. Nay, I don't tell you a Lye.

Miss. No, if you Lye, 'tis much.

'if you Lye, 'tis much' : either, 'If you lie, you tell a big one' or 'If you lie, you admit much'.

Nev. Well, I'm sure 'tis mine.

Miss. What, you think every Thing is yours; but a little the King has.

'you think every Thing is yours; but a little the King has' : *ODEP* cites this as a proverb. To me it sounds like an elaboration of the ironic 'A little the King has' or 'The King possesses a few things' addressed to a 'grab-all'.

Nev. Colonel, you have seen my fine Pick-Tooth Case: Don't you think this is the very same?

Col. Indeed, Miss, it is very like it.

Miss. Ay, what he says, you'll swear.

Nev. Well; but I'll prove it to be mine.

Miss. Ay, do if you can.

Nev. Why; what's yours is mine, and what's mine is my own.

> 'what's yours is mine, and what's mine is my own': compare 'What's mine is my own: what's my brother's is his and mine' (quoted by Fuller in 1732); both extend 'What's mine is mine (or, my) own', dating from *c.* 1600, if not earlier; yet even that may be a cynical perversion of the apparently yet earlier 'What's mine is yours, and what's yours is mine' (Apperson; *ODEP*).

Miss. Well, run on 'till you're weary, no Body holds you.

> 'run on 'till you're weary, no Body holds you': Talk until you're tired, nobody's stopping you.

[Neverout *gapes.*]

Col. What, Mr. *Neverout,* do you gape for Preferment?

> 'gape for Preferment': an oblique trenchancy, voiced by Swift rather than by the Colonel, on the preferment and patronage rife at the period.

Nev. Faith, I may gape long enough before it falls into my Mouth.

Lady Sm. Mr. *Neverout,* I hear you live high.

> 'I hear you live high': well and expensively.

Nev. Yes, Faith, Madam, live high, and lodge in a Garret.

> 'live high, and lodge in a Garret': a pun, of course; if Tom Neverout did, in fact, lodge in an attic, it was a comfortable one, not of the sort we associate with penniless poets.

Col. But, Miss, I forgot to tell you, that Mr. *Neverout* got the devilishest Fall in the Park To-Day.

> 'devilishest Fall': no one would dream of writing *devilishest* – and it's devilish hard to pronounce the word correctly.

Miss. I hope he did not hurt the Ground. But, how was it Mr. *Neverout?* I wish I had been there to laugh.

Nev. Why, Madam, it was a Place where a Cuckold had been bury'd, and one of his Horns sticking out, I happened to stumble against it. That was all.

> 'a Place where a Cuckold . . .': this seems to be Tom Neverout's own witticism or perhaps rather Swift's, so elaborate is it.

Lady Sm. Ladies, let us leave the Gentlemen to themselves; I think it is Time to go to our Tea.

Lady Answ. and *Miss.* My Lords, and Gentlemen, your most humble Servant.

Lord Sm. Well, Ladies, we'll wait on you an Hour hence.

[*The Gentlemen alone.*]

Lord Sm. Come, *John,* bring us a fresh Bottle.

Col. Ay, my Lord; and pray let him carry off the dead Men, (as we say in the Army.) [*Meaning the empty Bottles.*]

> 'carry off the dead Men, (as we say in the Army)' : this anticipation of the 19th–20th century *dead marines,* empty bottles (of liquor that has just been consumed), appears earliest in B.E.'s *Dictionary of the Canting Crew, c.* 1690, and persisted until *c.* 1890. The point is, that the *spirits have departed.*

Lord Sp. Mr. *Neverout,* pray is not that Bottle full?

Nev. Yes, my Lord, full of Emptiness.

> 'full of Emptiness' : this jocosity has survived. A species of adolescent wit.

Lord Sm. And, d'ye hear, *John,* bring clean Glasses.

Col. I'll keep mine, for I think the Wine is the best Liquor to wash Glasses in.

> 'Wine is the best Liquor to wash Glasses in' : ? only in Swift. *ODEP* records it as a proverb, and it may well have been one.

Third Conversation

[The Ladies at their Tea.]

Lady Smart

WELL, Ladies, now let us have a Cup of Discourse to our selves.

'a Cup of Discourse' : a cup of tea and the women's talk that goes with it. The ponderous *discourse* is intentional.

Lady Answ. What do you think of your Friend, Sir John *Spendall?*

Lady Sm. Why, Madam, 'tis happy for him that his Father was born before him.

'happy for him that his Father . . .' : a variant of 'Happy is he whose friends were born before him' (Ray, 1670) – said of a thriftless person.

Miss. They say, he makes a very ill Husband to my Lady.

Lady Ans. Well, but he must be allowed to be the fondest Father in the World.

Lady Sm. Ay, Madam, that's true; for they say, the Devil is kind to his own.

'the Devil is kind to his own' : with variant 'good' for 'kind', it goes back to *c.* 1600. The 19th–20th century version is : 'The Devil takes care of his own'.

Miss. I am told, my Lady manages him to Admiration.

'to Admiration' : astonishingly well.

Lady Sm. That I believe, for she's as cunning as a dead Pig; but not half so honest.

'as cunning as a dead Pig; . . . honest' : a proverb apparently recorded by Swift alone and certainly long obsolete. Without 'dead' it might have survived, for thus expressed it would have been much more trenchant.

Lady Answ. They say, she's quite a Stranger to all his Gallantries.

Lady Sm. Not at all; but you know, there's none so blind, as they that won't see.

'there's none so blind . . .' : 16th–20th centuries. Occasionally with addition : 'nor deaf as those who will not hear'.

Miss. Oh, Madam, I am told, she watches him as a Cat would watch a Mouse.

> 'watches him as a Cat . . .': mid 16th–20th centuries; usually '. . . as a cat watches . . .'

Lady Answ. Well, if she ben't foully bely'd; she pays him in his own Coyn.

> 'ben't foully bely'd': be not foully maligned.
> 'pays him in his own Coyn': a metaphor current since the 16th century or earlier.

Lady Sm. Madam, I fancy I know your Thoughts, as well, as if I were within you.

Lady Answ. Madam, I was t'other Day in Company with Mrs. *Clatter;* I find she gives her self Airs of being acquainted with your Ladyship.

> 'gives her self Airs of being acquainted with': fancies herself because she happens to have met.

Miss. O, the hideous Creature! Did you observe her Nails. They were long enough to scratch her Granum out of her Grave.

> 'Nails . . . long enough to scratch her Granum out of her Grave' (*granum* = *grannum* or *– am* = *grandam* = *grandame* = grandmother): probably 17th–20th centuries, but mostly rural in the 19th–20th. Apperson quotes a Yorkshire version cited by W. C. Hazlitt in 1860: 'Ye've nails at wad scrat [that would scratch] your granny out of her grave'.

Lady Sm. Well, she and *Tom Gosling* were banging Compliments backwards and forwards. It look'd like two Asses scrubbing one another.

> 'banging Compliments backwards and forwards': loudly exchanging exaggerated compliments.
> 'two Asses scrubbing one another': variation of the proverb, 'One mule (*or ass or horse*) doth scrub (*or scrubs*) another': 16th–19th centuries. Here, *scrub* = rub.

Miss. Ay, claw me, and I'll claw thee: But, pray Madam, who were the Company?

> 'claw me, and I'll claw thee': 16th–19th centuries. Nowadays: 'You scratch my back, and I'll scratch yours'.

Lady Sm. Why; there was all the World, and his Wife. There was Mrs. *Clatter,* Lady *Singular,* the Countess of *Talkham,* (I should have named her first) *Tom Goslin,* and some others, whom I have forgot.

'all the World, and his Wife' : a proverbial phrase apparently recorded first by Swift. The English North Country and Midlands have such jocular 19th–20th century variations as 'All the world and Bingham' – 'and Little Billing' – 'and part of Gateshead'. (Apperson.)

Lady Answ. I think the Countess is very sickly.

Lady Sm. Yes, Madam, she'll never scratch a grey Head, I promise her.

'She'll never scratch a grey Head' : never have one to scratch, never reach old age.

Miss. And pray, what was your Conversation?

Lady Sm. Why, Mrs. *Clatter* had all the Talk to her self, and was perpetually complaining of her Misfortunes.

Lady Answ. She brought her Husband ten thousand Pounds; she has a Town-House, and Country-House; would the Woman have her——hung with Points?

'would the Woman have her——hung with Points?' : Hasn't she enough to be proud of, does she want her breasts adorned with coverings made of thread lace? (Rather than points further south.)

Lady Sm. She would fain be at the Top of the House, before the Stairs are built.

'fain be at the Top of the House . . .' : expects to run before she can walk – in the world of Society.

Miss. Well, Comparisons are odious; but she's as like her Husband, as if she were spit out of his Mouth; as like as one Egg is to another. Pray, how was she drest?

'Comparisons are odious' : in English, since the 15th century; in Greek and Latin, since when?
'as like her Husband, as if . . .; as like as one Egg . . .' : the 'spit' simile probably dates from the 16th century – compare the later 'the very spit of (someone)'; the 'egg', from the early 16th century. The former is – except perhaps in dialect – obsolete; the latter, obsolescent.

Lady Sm. Why, she was as fine as Five-pence; but truly, I thought there was more Cost than Worship.

'fine as Five-pence' : a mid 16th–20th century simile; in the 19th–20th, increasingly rural. Compare :
'more Cost than Worship' : 18th–20th centuries; in the 19th–20th, mostly rural. (Apperson.) Much expense but little taste.

Lady Ans. I don't know her Husband; pray, what is he?

Lady Sm. Why, he's a Concealer of the Law; you must know, he came to us as drunk as *David's* Sow.

> 'a Concealer of the Law': 'a brilliant pun on "Counsellor"'
> (Saintsbury, 1892). Neat, yes; but brilliant? Short for *counsellor-at-law,* a barrister; archaic except in Ireland and the United States.
> 'as drunk as *David's* Sow': recorded in 1652, and already well established by 1671; probably of anecdotal origin; still quite common.

Miss. What kind of Creature is he?

Lady Sm. You must know the Man and his Wife are coupled like Rabits; a Fat and a Lean. He's as fat as a Porpoise, and she's one of *Pharaoh's* lean Kine. The Ladies, and *Tom Goslin,* were proposing a Party at *Quadrille,* but he refused to make one; damn your Cards, said he, they are the Devil's Books.

> 'coupled like Rabits; a Fat and a Lean': an allusion to the saying 'like a rabbit, fat and lean in four-and-twenty hours', used already in the first Dialogue.
> 'one of *Pharaoh's* lean Kine': an allusion to *Genesis,* chapter 41, and probably reminiscent of Shakespeare's description of thin persons as 'Pharaoh's lean kine'.
> 'Cards . . . the Devil's Books': mid-17th–20th centuries. Often paired with 'the Devil's bones' (dice).

Lady Ans. A dull, unmannerly Brute! Well, God send him more Wit, and me more Money.

> 'God send him more Wit . . . Money': a conversational shaping of the proverbial 'God send you more wit, and me more money', current since *c.* 1600.

Miss. Lord, Madam, I would not keep such Company for the World.

Lady Sm. O, Miss, 'tis nothing when you are used to it. Besides, you know; for Want of Company, welcome Trumpery.

> 'for Want of Company . . .': 1678, Ray; extant – but in 19th–20th centuries, mainly rural. Sometimes with logical 'good' before 'company' and at least once expressed as 'After company welcome trumpery'. (Apperson; *ODEP.*)

Miss. Did your Ladyship play?

Lady Sm. Yes, and won; so I came off with Fidler's Fare, Meat, Drink, and Money.

> 'Fidler's Fare . . .', with variants 'fee' and 'money', 'pay' and 'wages', and with slightly varying definitions, the proverbial

phrase goes back to late 16th century; since *c.* 1800, only among rustics.

Lady Ans. Ay, what says Pluck?

'what says Pluck?'. This is obscure. Apparently, however, Lady Answerall notices Miss Notable twitch and immediately remarks, consideringly, 'Ay, what says Pluck?' – What does that twitching mean?

Miss. Well, my Elbow itches, I shall change my Bed-fellow.

'my Elbow itches . . .': recorded earliest by Howell, 1659. Now folklore.

Lady Sm. And my Left-Hand itches, I shall receive Money.

'my Left-Hand itches . . .': folklore.

Lady Ans. And my Right-Eye itches, I shall cry.

'my Right-Eye itches . . .': either folklore or, more probably, a mere capping.

Lady Sm. Miss, I hear your Friend, Mrs. *Giddy*, has discarded *Dick Shuttle;* pray, has she got another Lover?

Miss. I hear of none.

Lady Sm. Why, the Fellow's rich, and I think she was a Fool, to throw out her dirty Water, before she got clean.

'a Fool, to throw out . . .': the proverb to which Lady Smart alludes is 'Don't throw away (*or* out) dirty water till you have got clean': 18th–19th centuries.

Lady Sm. Miss, that's a very handsome Gown of yours, and finely made, very genteel.

Miss. I'm glad your Ladyship likes it.

Lady Ans. Your Love will be in Raptures, it becomes you admirably.

Miss. Ay, I assure you, I won't take it as I have done, if this won't fetch him, the Devil fetch him, say I.

'if this won't fetch him . . .': I've done *my* best.

Lady Sm. [*To Lady* Answerall.] Pray, Madam, when did you see Sir *Peter Muckworm?*

Lady Ans. Not this Fortnight: I hear, he's laid up with the Gout.

Lady Sm. What does he do for it?

Lady Ans. Why, I hear he's weary of doctoring it, and now makes Use of nothing but Patience, and Flannel.

'Patience, and Flannel': 'What cannot be cured, must be endured' and at least one can keep warm.

Miss. Pray, how does he and my Lady agree?

Lady Ans. You know he loves her.——

> 'You know he loves her. – ' : should, I think, read '. . . her – ', with reference as in the almost too famous ending of Sterne's *Sentimental Journey*.

Miss. They say, she plays deep with Sharpers, that cheat her of her Money.

Lady Ans. Upon my Word, they must rise early that would cheat her of her Money. Sharp's the Word with her : Diamonds cut Diamonds.

> 'Upon my Word' : a still very general asseveration.
>
> 'they must rise early . . .' : the unit is *He* (or *They*) *must rise early who can* do something or other, especially to get the better of someone : 16th–20th centuries. (See, notably, Apperson.) Compare 'He must rise betimes who will cozen the Devil' : 17th–18th centuries.
>
> 'Sharp's the Word' : part catch-phrase, part proverbial saying : probably since late 17th century; usually with *sharp*=prompt, lively, very quick, but occasionally with *sharp*=shrewd. Compare the commercial slogan, 'Sharp's the word for toffee' (Sharp's Toffee).
>
> 'Diamonds cut Diamonds' : a variant of the 17th–20th century 'Diamond cut diamond'.

Miss. Well, but I was assured from a good Hand, that she lost at one Sitting, to the Tune of a hundred Guineas, make Money of that.

> 'to the Tune of' : to the sum or amount or number of. The *OED* records it for 1716.
>
> 'make Money of that' : and that's a considerable sum – that's a lot of money by any reckoning – that's not chicken-feed – an' that ain't hay.

Lady Sm. Well, but do you hear, that Mrs. *Plump* is brought to Bed at last?

Miss. And pray, what has God sent her?

> 'what has God sent her?' : boy or girl?

Lady Sm. Why, guess if you can.

Miss. A Boy, I suppose.

Lady Sm. No, you are out, guess again.

> 'you are out' : you are wrong.

Miss. A Girl then.

Lady Sm. You have hit it; I believe you are a Witch.

> 'You have hit it; . . . a Witch' : ironic. *ODEP* includes it; but *is it*

a proverb? A catch-phrase, perhaps. The 20th century equivalent is, 'How did you guess?'

Miss. O, Madam, the Gentlemen say, all fine Ladies are Witches; but I pretend to no such Thing.

'all fine Ladies are Witches' : a convention or a catch-phrase of the day; hardly a proverb. Since *c.* 1920, *witch* is a very common euphemism for *bitch* (of a woman), as in 'That —— oh, that *witch!*'

Lady Ans. Well, she had good Luck to draw *Tom Plump* into Wedlock; she rises with her——upwards.

'she rises with her——upwards' : 'arse' is probably the word.

Miss. Fye, Madam, what do you mean?
Lady Sm. O, Miss, 'tis nothing what we say among ourselves.

' 'tis nothing what we say among ourselves' : all girls together.

Miss. Ay, Madam, but they say, Hedges have Eyes, and Walls have Ears.

'Hedges have Eyes, and Walls have Ears' : the original is 'A field has eyes, and a wood has ears', as in a manuscript of *c.* 1225 and again in Chaucer, *c.* 1386; by the 16th century, it had become 'Fields have eyes, and woods have ears', predominant also in the 17th, popular in the 18th and 19th, nor entirely unknown in the 20th. From that double proverb, sprang the 'Walls have ears' version, adumbrated in the 16th and well established by the early 17th, and now much commoner than the original. (Based upon the enlightening entries in Apperson and *ODEP*.)

Lady Ans. Well, Miss, I can't help it; you know I am old Tell-truth, I love to call a Spade, a Spade.

'Tell-truth' : an inveterately truthful and invincibly frank person; current in mid-16th–mid-19th centuries.
'call a Spade, a Spade' and neither 'a garden implement' nor 'a bloody shovel' : recorded in 1519 and having its original in Erasmus's *ficus ficus, ligonem ligonem vocat,* he calls figs figs, and a hoe a hoe.

[*Lady* Smart *mistakes the Tea-Tongs for a Spoon.*]
Lady Sm. What, I think my Wits are a Wooll-gathering To-Day.

'my Wits are a Wooll-gathering' (now '. . . are wool-gathering') : 'I'm absent-minded or day-dreaming' : 16th–20th centuries.

Miss. Why, Madam, there was but a Right, and a Wrong.
Lady Sm. Miss, I hear that you and Lady *Couplers,* are as great as Cup, and Can.

'as great as Cup, and Can' : very intimate or constantly together :
16th–early 19th centuries. Either the cup from which the liquor is
drunk and the can from which it is poured, or, less probably, wine-
cup and beer-can.

Lady Ans. Ay, as great as the Devil, and the Earl of *Kent.*

'as great as the Devil, and the Earl of *Kent*' : very closely
associated : late 17th–18th century. Earl Godwin, who died in
1053, was, according to history, a villainous character.

Lady Sm. Nay, I am told you meet together with as much Love,
as there is between the old Cow and the Hay-Stack.

'with as much Love, as . . . between the old Cow . . .' : much love :
apparently recorded only here, this rural proverb could be very
old.

Miss. I own, I love her very well; but there's Difference betwixt
staring and stark mad.

'there's Difference between staring and stark mad' : in the 16th
century, it was 'blind', not 'mad'; the 'mad' version, however,
appears in print as early as 1616 (*ODEP*) and is not yet obsolete.

Lady Sm. They say, she begins to grow fat.

Miss. Fat, ay, fat as a Hen in the Forehead.

'fat as a Hen in the Forehead' : not fat at all : 17th–19th centuries. Compare the role of the hen in *hen-witted,* brainless.

Lady Sm. Indeed, Lady *Answerall,* (pray forgive me) I think your
Ladyship looks a little thinner, than when I saw you last.

Miss. Indeed, Madam, I think not; but your Ladyship is one of
Job's Comforters.

'one of *Job's* Comforters' : a comforter tending to make things
worse. From the Biblical book of *Job,* xvi, 1–2.

Lady Ans. Well, no Matter how I look; I am bought and sold. But
really, Miss, you are so very obliging, that I wish I were a handsome
young Lord for your Sake.

'I am bought and sold' : betrayed; here, perhaps merely deserted
momentarily by my friends; 14th–18th centuries; then rare; then,
by 1900, obsolescent.

Miss. O, Madam, your Love's a Million.

'your Love's a Million' : you are *much* too kind. Compare the 20th
century mostly American slang 'Thanks a million!' : here, as
there, *a million* is a mere intensive.

Lady Sm. [*To Lady* Answerall.] Madam, will your Ladyship let me
wait on you to the Play To-morrow.

Lady Ans. Madam, it becomes me to wait on your Ladyship.
Miss. What, then I'm turn'd out for a Wrangler.

> 'turn'd out for a Wrangler' : passed by or set aside or discarded as
> an argumentative person.

[*The Gentlemen come in to the Ladies, to drink Tea.*]
Miss. Mr. *Neverout,* we wanted you sadly; you are always out of
the Way, when you should be hang'd.

> 'always out of the Way, when you should be hang'd' : perhaps not
> itself a proverb, but Miss Notable's playful variation of 'always in
> the lane when you should be in the field' (or *vice versa*) : never
> where you're wanted.

Nev. You wanted me? Pray, Miss, how do you look, when you lye?
Miss. Better than you when you cry, Manners indeed. I find, you
mend like sower Ale in Summer.

> 'how do you look, when you lye? – Better than you when you cry' :
> a jingle.
> 'you mend like sower Ale in Summer' : improve no more than sour
> ale does in summer, when, of course, it deteriorates : 16th–19th
> (? 20th) centuries, often with 'as' for 'like'.

Nev. I beg your Pardon, Miss; I only meant, when you lye alone.

> 'when you lye alone' : when you are in bed alone. Another of the
> multitudinous puns on the two verbs *lie*.

Miss. That's well turn'd; one Turn more would have turn'd you
down Stairs.

> 'one turn more . . .' : another 'dirty crack' and you'd have been
> out on your ear.

Nev. Miss, come be kind for once, and order me a Dish of Coffee.
Miss. Pray, go yourself; let us wear out the oldest first. Besides, I
can't go, for I have a Bone in my Leg.

> 'I can't go, for I have a Bone in my Leg' : the 18th–20th century
> form of an excuse that, in the 16th, was usually 'in the throat' and,
> in the 17th–18th, often 'in the arm'; as Ray said in 1678, it 'is a
> pretended excuse' or a humorous one. Upon that traditional sense
> there has been superimposed another, described by Saintsbury, in
> 1892, as 'a peculiar cramp in the leg' and, in 19th–20th century
> rural lore, as 'a shooting pain in the (arm or) leg'. Apperson.

Col. They say, a Woman need but once look on her Apron Strings
to find an Excuse.

> 'a Woman need but once look . . . Excuse' : with variant 'apron

string', this proverb was current throughout the 17th–18th centuries.

Nev. Why, Miss, you are grown so peevish, a Dog would not live with you.

'so peevish, a Dog . . .': Neverout's own, apparently.

Miss. Mr. *Neverout,* no Offence I hope; but, truly, I think, in a little Time, you intend to make the Colonel as bad as your self; and that's as bad as bad can be.

'as bad as bad can be': one of the most frequent tunes played on the theme, 'as – as – can be', which is also a syntactical pattern.

Nev. My Lord; don't you think Miss improves wonderfully of late? Why, Miss, if I spoil the Colonel, I hope you will use him as you do me; for you know, love me, love my Dog.

'love me, love my Dog': 15th–20th centuries. Compare St Bernard's 12th century aphorism, *Qui me amat, amat et canem meum,* He who loves me, loves my dog also.

Col. How's that, *Tom?* say that again. Why, if I am a Dog, shake Hands Brother.

'if I am a Dog, shake Hands Brother': one of the animal-human group of witticisms patterned by 'Good morning, mother of *asses.* – Good morning, my *son.*'

[*Here a great, loud and long Laugh.*]

Lord Sm. But, pray Gentlemen, why always so severe upon poor Miss. On my Conscience, Colonel, and *Tom Neverout,* one of you two are both Knaves.

'On my Conscience': *by my conscience* in Middle English; *on* or *upon* . . ., Middle-Modern English: an asseveration originally solemn.

'one of you two are both Knaves': both of you are knaves. This remark belongs to the group of trenchantly illogical witticisms of the kind exemplified by 'There are two fools born every minute, and he is all three of them'.

Col. My Lady *Answerall,* I intend to do my self the Honour of dining with your Ladyship To-morrow.

Lady Ans. Ay, Colonel, do if you can.

Miss. I'm sure you'll be glad to be welcome.

'you'll be glad to be welcome': for, after all, 'He that is welcome fares well' – as an 18th century proverb has it.

Col. Miss, I thank you; and to reward you, I'll come and drink Tea with you in the Morning.

Miss. Colonel, there's two Words to that Bargain.

> 'there's two Words to that Bargain' : we've heard yours; but what about *mine*? The basic proverb is 'Two words to a bargain' : late 16th–mid-19th centuries.

Col. [*To Lady* Smart.] Your Ladyship has a very fine Watch; well may you wear it.

> 'well may you wear it' : elegantly and for many years.

Lady Sm. It is none of mine, Colonel.

Col. Pray, whose is it then?

Lady Sm. Why 'tis my Lord's; for, they say, a marry'd Woman has nothing of her own, but her Wedding-Ring, and her Hair-Lace. But if Women had been the Law-Makers, it would have been better.

> 'marry'd Woman has nothing . . .' : classified by *ODEP* as a proverb, and probably it was.

Col. This Watch seems to be quite new.

Lady Sm. No, Sir, it has been twenty Years in my Lord's Family, but *Quare* lately put a new Case and Dial-Plate to it.

> 'Quare lately put a new Case . . .' : Saintsbury comments thus, 'Daniel Q., died in 1724. He had invented repeaters, and throughout the eighteenth century was what Tompion was later among watchmakers, what Joe Manton long was among gunmakers, a name to conjure with and to quote'.

Nev. Why, that's for all the World like the Man, who swore he kept the same Knife for forty Years, only he sometimes changed the Haft, and sometimes the Blade.

> 'swore he kept the same Knife for forty Years . . .' : anecdotal.

Lord Sm. Well, *Tom,* to give the Devil his due, thou art a right Woman's Man.

> 'to give the Devil his due' : mid-16th–20th centuries. At first literal, it soon came to mean 'to give one's enemy, or merely a person one dislikes, his due'.
>
> 'a right Woman's Man' : a real or proper one; better, eminently one. Nowadays, where the Cockney says 'a proper so-and-so', the Yorkshireman says 'a reet one'.

Col. Od so, I have broke the Hinge of my Snuff-Box, I'm undone, beside the Loss.

Miss. A-lack-a-Day, Colonel, I vow I had rather have found forty Shillings.

> 'I had rather have found forty Shillings' : In your place, I should rather have found that sum. Ironic.

Nev. Why, Colonel; all I can say, to comfort you, is, that you must mend it with a new one.

> 'mend it with a new one': make good the loss by getting a new one. If Tom Neverout had put his mind to it, he could have become a notable wit.

[*Miss laughs.*]

Col. What, Miss, you can't laugh, but you must shew your Teeth.

Miss. I'm sure, you shew your Teeth, when you can't bite. Well, thus it must be, if we sell Ale.

> 'you shew your Teeth, when you can't bite': you talk fiercely, but act mildly. A variation of 'Never show your teeth if you cannot (*or* can't) bite': 17th–20th centuries; now seldom heard.
> 'Thus it must be, if we sell Ale': a variation of 'This' – or 'Such things' – 'must be if we brew (*or* sell) ale': mid-17th–mid-19th century. We must abide by the conditions of our trade or profession; hence, by the results of our actions.

Nev. Miss, you smell very sweet: I hope, you don't carry Perfumes.

> 'carry Perfumes': use them on your person when you go out visiting (etc.): compare the 20th century American 'wear perfumes'.

Miss. Perfumes! No, Sir, I'd have you to know, it is nothing but the Grain of my Skin.

Lord Sp. So, Ladies, and Gentlemen, methinks you are very witty upon one another: Come, box it about, 'twill come to my Father at last.

> 'witty upon one another': at one another's expense.
> 'box it about, 'twill come to my Father at last': 'The famous Jacobite cant-phrase for breeding disturbance in hopes of a fresh Revolution' – says George Saintsbury. But Aubrey, *Brief Lives*, has it, in the frequent variant 'give it about . . .', in 1680, concerning the young Walter Raleigh and a buffet given him by his father. Kelly, 1721, explains the saying as: 'Spoken when we would have some ill turn done to somebody, but not immediately by ourself'. (See especially *The Oxford Book of Quotations* and . . . *of Proverbs*.)

Col. Why, my Lord, you see Miss has no Mercy, I wish she were marry'd; but I doubt, the grey Mare would prove the better Horse.

> 'The grey Mare . . .': The proverb 'The grey mare is . . .' (The wife rules the husband) goes back to *c*. 1500.

Miss. Well, God forgive you for that Wish.

Lord Sp. Never fear him, Miss.

Lord Sm. What have you to say to that, Colonel?

Nev. O, my Lord, my Friend, the Colonel, scorns to set his Wit against a Child.

'scorns to set his wit' : the proverb 'Don't set your wit against a child' has occurred in the first Dialogue.

Miss. Scornful Dogs will eat dirty Puddens.

'Scornful Dogs will eat dirty Puddens' : with variant 'Hungry' for 'Scornful', the proverb covers the 16th–20th centuries; in the 19th–20th, mostly rural and dialectal.

Col. Well, Miss, they say, a Woman's Tongue is the last Thing about her that dyes : Therefore, let's kiss and Friends.

'a Woman's Tongue . . .' : 17th–19th centuries. In 1612, 'Homer' Chapman most movingly wrote, 'When a man dies, the last thing that moves is his heart; in a woman, her tongue'. (Apperson.)

'let's kiss and Friends' : not an error for 'kiss and be friends', as we see from Quarles's 'Come, buss [=kiss] and friends' (1635), although 'and be friends' is, naturally enough, much the commoner form, recorded (*ODEP*) for 1300, and probably occurring still earlier. Long since weakened to mean 'become friends again'.

Miss. Hands off.

Lord Sp. Faith, Colonel, you are in for Ale, and Cakes. But, after all, Miss, you are too severe; you would not meddle with your Match?

'Ale, and Cakes' : a reversal of 'cakes and ale' – good healthy eating and drinking. In Shakespeare's *Twelfth Night*, Sir Toby neatly asks a puritanical fellow, 'Dost thou think, because thou art virtuous, there shall be no more cakes and ale?'

'meddle with your Match?' : cross swords, or spar, with your equal in wit.

Miss. All they can say, goes in at one Ear, and out at t'other for me, I can assure you; only, I wish they would be quiet, and let me drink my Tea.

'All . . . goes in at one Ear . . .' : adumbrated, *c.* 1374, by Chaucer and recorded, 1546, by Heywood. To take no notice of what is said.

Nev. What, I warrant you think all is lost that goes beside your own Mouth.

Miss. Pray, Mr. *Neverout*, hold your Tongue for once, if it be possible. Women! One would think you were a Woman in Men's Cloaths, by your prating.

'Women!' : You men talk about women; but . . .

Nev. No, Miss, it is not handsome to see one hold one's Tongue; besides, I should slobber my Fingers.

'not handsome to see . . .' : unseemly.

Col. Miss, did you never hear, that three Women, and a Goose, are enough to make a Market.

'three Women, and a Goose' : known as a proverb as early as 1586; in the 19th–20th centuries, mostly rural. Miss parries this very neatly with her '. . . make a Fair' (even noisier).

Miss. I'm sure, if Mr. *Neverout,* or you, were among them, it would make a Fair.

[Footman comes in.]

Lady Sm. Here, take away the Tea-Table, and bring up Candles.

Lady Ans. O, Madam, no Candles yet, I beseech you; don't let us burn Day-Light.

'burn Day-Light' : use artificial light while natural light is still good, French *brûler des bougies – des lampes,* etc. – *en plein jour.* Current ever since *c.* 1550; a couple of times in Shakespeare; indeed, for some reason, very common among the dramatists of *c.* 1560–1730. (Apperson.)

Nev. I dare swear; Miss, for her Part, will never burn Day-Light, if she can help it.

Miss. Lord, Mr. *Neverout,* one can't hear ones own Ears for you.

'one can't hear ones own Ears for you' : you deafen one with your constant talk.

Lady Sm. Indeed, Madam, it is blind Man's Holiday, we shall soon be all of a Colour.

'blind Man's Holiday' : twilight, or an otherwise very bad light. A proverbial phrase of the late 16th–20th centuries.
'all of a Colour' : for, 'in the dark, all cats are grey' or 'Joan is as good as my lady in the dark', proverbs with Greek and Latin originals. Neverout's comment is ambiguous : presumably he means 'kiss whom we please'.

Nev. Why then, Miss, we may kiss where we like best.

Miss. Fogh, these Men talk of nothing but kissing.

[She spits.]

Nev. What, Miss, does it make your Mouth water?

'make your Mouth water?' : since at least as early as 1650.

Lady Sm. It is as good to be in the Dark, as without Light; therefore, pray bring in Candles. They say, Women, and Linnen, shew best by Candle-Light. Come, Gentlemen, are you for a Party at *Quadrille?*

'as good to be in the Dark . . .' : a sort of nonsensical catch-phrase, occurring in Ray, 1670.
'Women, and Linnen . . .' : 18th–20th centuries; after *c.* 1800, mostly rural. I suspect that this is a conscious reversal of the mid-16th–18th (? 19th) century proverb, 'Choose not a woman nor linen' – or 'neither . . . nor' – 'by candle-light'.

Col. I'll make one, with you three Ladies.
Lady Ans. I'll sit down, and be a Stander-by.

'sit down . . . a Stander-by' : an unconscious 'bull'. All her Ladyship means is that she'll look on.

Lord Sm. [*To Lady* Answerall.] Madam, does your Ladyship never play?
Col. Yes, I suppose, her Ladyship plays sometimes for an Egg at *Easter.*
Never. Ay, and a Kiss at *Christmas.*

'plays . . . for an Egg at *Easter.* – Ay, and a kiss at *Christmas.*' Perhaps an 'Easter egg' and 'under the mistletoe'. Ray, 1670, has 'I will warrant you for an egg at Easter'; the Denham Tracts, 1846–59, have 'a kiss at Christmas and an egg at Easter' : customary greeting and customary gift.

Lady Ans. Come, Mr. *Neverout,* hold your Tongue, and mind your Knitting.

'hold your Tongue . . .' : hold your tongue and mind your own business. Perhaps reminiscent of the mid-17th–18th century 'hold your tongue, husband, and let me talk that have all the wit'.

Nev. With all my Heart. Kiss my Wife, and welcome.

'Kiss my Wife, and welcome' : part of the proverb cited by Kelly, 1721, as 'Contentibus, quoth Tommy Tomson, kiss my wife and welcome' (*contentibus* is mock-Latin for 'I'm *content*') – with the gloss, 'Spoken facetiously when we comply with a project'.

[*The Colonel, Mr.* Neverout, *Lady* Smart, *and Miss, go to* Quadrille, *and sit 'till Three in the Morning.*] [*They rise from Cards.*]
Lady Sm. Well, Miss, you'll have a sad Husband, you have such good Luck at Cards.

'You'll have a sad Husband . . .' : a variation upon the theme, 'unlucky in love, lucky at play' (*or* 'cards') : late 17th–20th century.

Nev. Indeed, Miss, you dealt me sad Cards; if you deal so ill by your Friends, what will you do with your Enemies?

> 'if you deal so ill by your Friends . . .': perhaps compare that ancient saying which apparently goes back to the 3rd century BC and which has numerous variations of the pattern, 'I can deal with my enemies, but God save me from my friends!'

Lady Ans. I'm sure, 'tis Time for all honest Folks to go to Bed.

> ''tis Time for all honest Folks . . .': cited by *ODEP* as proverbial.

Miss. Indeed, my Eyes draw Straws. [*she's almost asleep.*]

> 'my Eyes draw Straws': I feel drowsy: late 17th–20th centuries; in 19th–20th rural. Variants: 'pick' or 'gather'.

Nev. Why, Miss, if you fall asleep, some Body may get a Pair of Gloves.

> 'a Pair of Gloves': in return for a stolen kiss. A very old piece of folklore.

Col. I'm going to the Land of Nod.

> 'the Land of Nod': the land of folk asleep; that is, sleep. Late 17th–20th centuries. By a pun on *Genesis,* iv, 16, 'Then Cain went away . . . and dwelt in the land of Nod, east of Eden' – literally, the Land of Wandering.

Nev. Faith, I'm for *Bedfordshire.*

> Bedfordshire': a pun on 'bed'. Used by dramatist Middleton in 1608. Extant.

Lady Sm. I'm sure, I shall sleep without rocking.

> 'sleep without rocking': without being rocked in a cradle. It occurs as early as 1631; obsolete by 1900. (Apperson.)

Nev. Miss, I hope you'll dream of your Sweetheart.

Miss. O, no doubt of it: I believe, I shan't be able to sleep for dreaming of him.

> 'dream of your Sweetheart': probably implying himself. Miss, in turn, implies that her sleep will be dreamless.

Col. [*To Miss.*] Madam, I shall have the Honour to escorte you.

Miss. No, Colonel, I thank you. My Mama, has sent her Chair, and Footmen. Well, my Lady *Smart,* I'll give you Revenge whenever you please.

> 'My Mama': in the 18th century, an upper-class form of reference, as 'Mama' (*or* 'Mamma') was of address.
>
> 'give you your Revenge': a return game of cards. Wycherley, 1672. (*OED*).

[*Footman comes in.*]

Footman. Madam, the Chairs are waiting.

'the Chairs' : sedan-chairs, introduced into England – from Italy – in 1634. (The *OED* has a valuable historical note on *sedan* and the synonymous *chair*.)

[*They all take their Chairs, and go off.*]

FINIS.

INDEX OF SUBJECTS

including Persons and Book-Titles

To supply an index of the catch-phrases, proverbs, slang words and archaic forms, commented on by Swift in his Introduction and exemplified by him in the Dialogues, would be to compile a work almost as large as the original. I have rested content with a list of the general subjects and the names and titles mentioned in the two introductions; in the few instances where the Dialogues touch on a general subject, whether already treated or not, the reference is made.

abbreviating : 27, 33, 45
academies : 12
affectation : 45
Apperson, G. L. : 9
Arbuthnot, John : 37, 47

'bargains' and 'bites' : 28–29, 37, 44
Brown, Thomas : 37, 46–47
Burnet, Bishop Gilbert : 27

'cant' (=fashionable slang) words : 26–27, 33, 43, 45–46
cards : 34, 35, 46
catch-phrases : 15, 16
Cibber, Colley : 39, 41, 47
clichés : 16
coarseness : 30, 32
colloquialisms : 15, 16, 18, 45
Craftsman, The : 38, 47
crambo, the : 66
Creech, Thomas : 22, 43

Davis, Herbert : 9, 13, 14, 15
Dennis, John : 37, 47
Derbyshire dialect : 17, 36
dialect in general : 33, 45, 46
dinner : 34
Discourse to Prove the Antiquity . . . , A : 11, 13
Dobrée, Bonamy : 16

dramatis personae of the Dialogues : 17, 52
Dryden : 11

enthusiasm : 29, 44
Essay on Conversation, An : 13–14

free-thinking : 28–29, 44

Gay, John : 37, 47
gestures : 24–25, 32, 43
Gildon, Charles : 37, 47
grammar : 18, 33, 45
Grimston, Viscount : 75

Harvey, Sir Paul : 9
Hobbes, Thomas : 46

identification of shadowy persons : 26–27, 43–44
illiteracies : 16, 45
innuendo : 44
irony : 17
Isaac, the dancing-master : 25, 43

jargon : 25, 43

Letter to a Young Clergyman, A : 12

life-like dialogue : 17–18, 33–34
Lilly, William : 33, 45

Newton, Isaac : 41, 47–48

oaths : 18, 30–31, 32, 44
orthography : 33, 45
*Oxford Dictionary of English
    Proverbs, The* : 9
*Oxford English Dictionary,
    The* : 9
Ozell, John : 37, 47

Perrot, Sir John : 31, 45
Polite Conversation, remarks
    upon : 13, 14–18
Pope, Alexander : 37, 47
Proposal for Correcting . . ., A :
    11, 12
proverbs : 9, 15, 16, 23–24
puns : 47

repartees : 15, 23, 24, 34, 42, 48
romances : 32, 45

Saintsbury, George : 11, 12, 13,
    16, 17, 43
slang. See 'cant'
spleen, the : 22, 43
Stevens, John : 37, 47
Sutherland, James : 16
Swift's contribution to study of
    English : 9, 17–18
Swift's prose style : 9, 11
Swift's retentive and delicate
    ear : 9

The Tatler, No. 230 : 11–12, 14
tea : 26, 28, 32, 38
Theobald, Lewis : 39, 41–42, 47

Wagstaff and Bickerstaff : 14
Ward, Edward : 37, 47
wit : 15, 16, 26, 28, 34, 36
women in conversation : 13–14,
    23, 28, 30

Young, Edward (the poet) : 37,
    47

Other works by the editor

Published by Messrs Routledge & Kegan Paul Ltd:

ORIGINS: An Etymological Dictionary of Modern English, with appendices of prefixes, suffixes, roots. 3rd edition, much revised and somewhat enlarged; 90s. (U.S.: The Macmillan Company; $16.00.)

A DICTIONARY OF THE UNDERWORLD, BRITISH AND AMERICAN. 2nd edition, revised and enlarged; 70s. (U.S.: Macmillan; $12.00.)

A DICTIONARY OF SLANG AND UNCONVENTIONAL ENGLISH. 5th edition, revised and much-enlarged, in 2 vols.; 105s. the set. (U.S.: Macmillan; $16.00.)

A SMALLER SLANG DICTIONARY: 20th century only; suitable for homes and schools. 18s. (U.S.: Macmillan; $3.50.)

SLANG TODAY AND YESTERDAY: A History and a Study. 3rd edition, 3rd impression; 42s. (U.S.: Macmillan; $7.00.)

A DICTIONARY OF CLICHÉS, with an introduction. 4th edition, 3rd impression; 12s. 6d. (U.S.: Macmillan; $2.50.)

COMIC ALPHABETS: historical and analytical and light-hearted. Illustrated by Michael Foreman, 12s. 6d.

Published by Messrs Hamish Hamilton Ltd:

USAGE AND ABUSAGE: A Guide to Good English. 5th edition (revised, enlarged, brought up to date), 3rd impression; 21s. (U.S.: The British Book Centre, New York City; $5.25.)

THE CONCISE USAGE AND ABUSAGE. 3rd impression; 10s. 6d. (U.S.: British Book Centre; $2.75.)

A CHARM OF WORDS: essays on language. 2nd edition; 15s. (U.S.: Macmillan; $3.50.)

FROM SANSKRIT TO BRAZIL: essays on language. 10s. 6d. (U.S.: British Book Centre; $2.25.)

NAME THIS CHILD: A Dictionary of given or Christian names. 5th edition – but the first in this abridgement; 5s. (U.S.: British Book Centre; $1.50.)

WHAT'S THE MEANING?: An Introduction to Etymology for Young People and Other Beginners. 4th impression; 10s. 6d. (U.S.: British Book Centre; $2.25.)

A FIRST BOOK OF QUOTATIONS, with introduction and

indexes. 2nd edition, revised; 12*s.* 6*d.* (U.S.: British Book Centre; $3.25.)

YOU HAVE A POINT THERE: A Guide to Punctuation and Its Allies, with an American chapter by John W. Clark. 4th edition, 3rd impression; 15*s.* (U.S.: British Book Centre; $3.50.)

Published by Basil Blackwell & Mott Ltd:

NOTES ON PUNCTUATION. 3rd edition; 1*s.* 6*d.* Compact and thorough.

Published by Messrs Faber & Faber Ltd:

THE 'SHAGGY DOG' STORY: a brief history, with many seemly examples, illustrated by V. H. Drummond. 3rd impression; 7*s.* 6*d.* (U.S.: British Book Centre; $2.25.)

Published by André Deutsch Ltd:

ADVENTURING AMONG WORDS: a light-hearted excursion in etymology. 2nd edition; 10*s.* 6*d.* (U.S.: The Oxford University Press, Inc.; $2.75.)

Published by Macdonald & Company (Publishers) Ltd:

ENGLISH: A COURSE FOR HUMAN BEINGS. 5th edition: 1-vol. edition, 25*s.*; 3-vol. edition (Elementary; Middle; Advanced) —9*s.* 6*d.* each. (U.S.: British Book Centre: $6.00; $2.50 each.)